Literacy by Design™

Assessment Guide

Theme Progress Tests and Test Practice

Rigby®

A Harcourt Achieve Imprint

www.Rigby.com

1-800-531-5015

Contents

Using This Book

Ongoing Test Practice

Ongoing Test Practice provides students with reading passages and questions to practice the current theme's skills.

- Give the Ongoing Test Practice as homework after Lesson 7 of each theme.
- Make a transparency of the passage and questions to do more in-depth standardized test practice.
- Use the Answer Key on page 176 of this book to score Ongoing Test Practice.

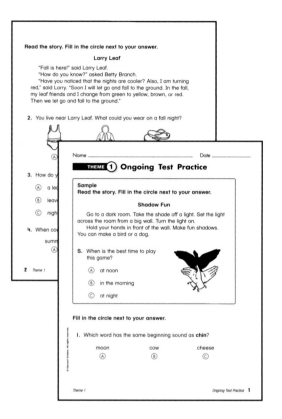

Theme Progress Tests

Theme Progress Tests cover skills and content from the student materials for each theme: comprehension, target skills, vocabulary, phonics, writing, and grammar.

- Administer the Theme Progress Test on the last day of each theme.
- Use the Student Test Record to determine students' scores using the answer key provided. Use reteaching suggestions provided at the end of each test if students score below the criterion score.

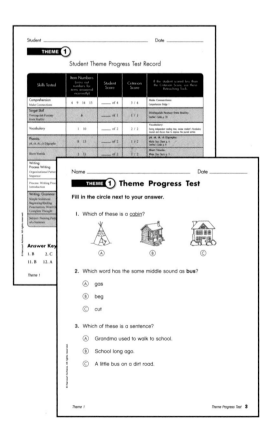

Mid-Year and End-of-Year Reviews

The Mid-Year and End-of-Year Reviews provide cumulative assessments. Students practice taking tests using new reading passages.

- The Student Test Record at the end of each test allows for easy scoring and provides reteaching suggestions.

High-Frequency Word Assessments

High-Frequency Word Assessments test the child's recognition of the current theme's high-frequency words. In second grade, high-frequency words are covered in the first ten themes.

- Administer the High-Frequency Word Assessment at the end of each theme.
- Use the High-Frequency Word Assessment Tracking Form on page 175 to record the words students did not recognize and make notes about student responses.

Using Rigby READS for Reading Level Placement

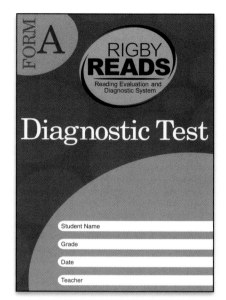

Ease of Student Placement

The Rigby READS (Reading Evaluation and Diagnostic System) is a valid and reliable assessment that can be administered to the whole class in a single day. On the basis of this quick and easy assessment, teachers receive the following information.

- **Placement** Each student's individual reading level for initial instruction

- **Diagnostic** A five-pillar diagnostic that pinpoints strengths and development areas in comprehension, phonics, phonemic awareness, fluency, and vocabulary

This invaluable resource is built right into the *Literacy by Design* program. Forms A and B allow you to determine end-of-year progress. The chart below shows how the Rigby READS reading levels correlate to the *Literacy by Design* reading levels.

Rigby READS Reading Level Correlation

Rigby READS Reading Level	*Literacy by Design* Reading Level	Rigby READS Reading Level	*Literacy by Design* Reading Level
Early Readiness	A	2.4	M
Kindergarten	B	3.1	N
1.1	C	3.2	O
1.2	D	3.3	P
1.3	E	4.1	Q
1.4	F	4.2	R
1.5	G	4.3	S
1.6	H	5.1	T
1.7	I	5.2	U
2.1	J	5.2	V
2.2	K	6.1	W
2.3	L		

Filling in a Circle

On a test, you may need to fill in a circle. This is how you show your answer. Fill in the circle next to the best answer. Fill in the circle completely.

Look at the circles on this page. Only the first one shows the right way to fill in an answer circle.

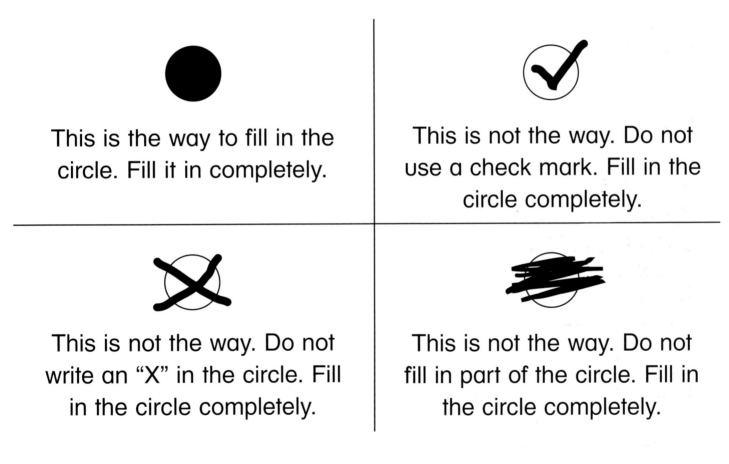

This is the way to fill in the circle. Fill it in completely.

This is not the way. Do not use a check mark. Fill in the circle completely.

This is not the way. Do not write an "X" in the circle. Fill in the circle completely.

This is not the way. Do not fill in part of the circle. Fill in the circle completely.

Let's Practice!

I. Fill in the circle next to the **house**.

Ⓐ   Ⓑ   Ⓒ

2. Fill in the circle next to the **door**.

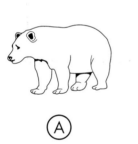 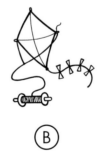 

Ⓐ   Ⓑ   Ⓒ

3. Fill in the circle next to the **kite**.

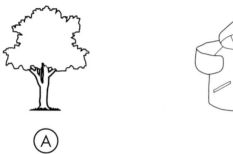  

Ⓐ   Ⓑ   Ⓒ

4. Fill in the circle next to the **cow**.

Ⓐ   Ⓑ   Ⓒ

Name _____   Date _____

THEME 1 Ongoing Test Practice

Sample
Read the story. Fill in the circle next to your answer.

Shadow Fun

Go to a dark room. Take the shade off a light. Set the light across the room from a big wall. Turn the light on.

Hold your hands in front of the wall. Make fun shadows. You can make a bird or a dog.

S. When is the best time to play this game?

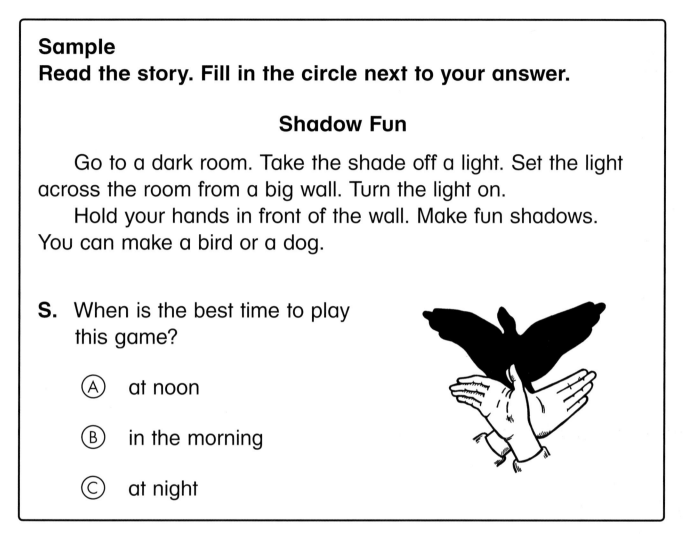

Ⓐ   at noon

Ⓑ   in the morning

Ⓒ   at night

Fill in the circle next to your answer.

I. Which word has the same beginning sound as **chin**?

      moon   cow   cheese
       Ⓐ   Ⓑ   Ⓒ

Read the story. Fill in the circle next to your answer.

Larry Leaf

"Fall is here!" said Larry Leaf.

"How do you know?" asked Betty Branch.

"Have you noticed that the nights are cooler? Also, I am turning red," said Larry. "Soon I will let go and fall to the ground. In the fall, my leaf friends and I change from green to yellow, brown, or red. Then we let go and fall to the ground."

2. You live near Larry Leaf. What could you wear on a fall night?

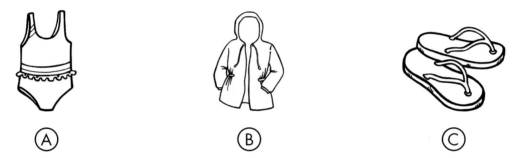

Ⓐ   Ⓑ   Ⓒ

3. How do you know this story is a fantasy?

Ⓐ   a leaf talks

Ⓑ   leaves change colors

Ⓒ   nights get cooler

4. When could you take photos of trees with brightly colored leaves?

summer   fall   winter

Ⓐ   Ⓑ   Ⓒ

Name _____   Date _____

THEME 1 Theme Progress Test

Fill in the circle next to your answer.

I. Which of these is a <u>cabin</u>?

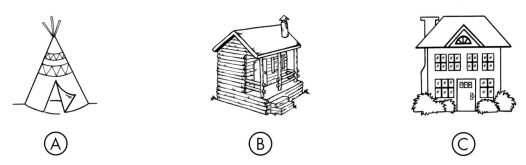

Ⓐ A Ⓑ B Ⓒ C

2. Which word has the same middle sound as **bus**?

Ⓐ gas

Ⓑ beg

Ⓒ cut

3. Which of these is a sentence?

Ⓐ Grandma used to walk to school.

Ⓑ School long ago.

Ⓒ A little bus on a dirt road.

4. Read the lines from "The Soda Shop."

> The radio played the latest hits.
> The kids all danced for hours.
> When I go to sleep at night,
> I dream that I am there.

When can kids listen and dance to music today?

Ⓐ   when they go to a school party

Ⓑ   when they take a math test

Ⓒ   when they eat lunch

5. What is the naming part of the sentence in the box?

> Carol played on the slide.

Ⓐ   played

Ⓑ   Carol

Ⓒ   slide

6. Read the lines from "Asha in the Attic."

So, while Grandpa was snoozing out in the sun, Asha crept back into the house. She tiptoed up and up the stairs.

What could you add to make this story a fantasy?

Ⓐ The stairs began to move and talk.

Ⓑ Asha went into the attic.

Ⓒ Grandpa woke up from his nap.

7. Which sentence would best start a story?

Ⓐ Next Max played a song.

Ⓑ Finally Max took a bow.

Ⓒ First Max sat at the piano.

8. Which word has the same ending sound as **with**?

Ⓐ wish

Ⓑ bath

Ⓒ bench

9. Read the lines from "The Soda Shop."

> My great-grandpa's soda shop
> Was the coolest spot in town,
> With shiny floors and a turning door
> That spun like a merry-go-round.

What else spins like a merry-go-round?

(A) the glass in a window

(B) the pages of a book

(C) the wheel of a bike

10. Choose the word that goes on the line.

The sisters are twins. They are the same age. They are in the same _____ of the Jackson family.

(A) visit

(B) generation

(C) tradition

11. Which picture name has the same middle sound as **deck**?

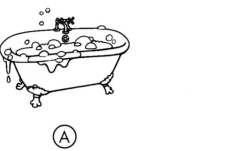
Ⓐ

Ⓑ

Ⓒ

12. Which step goes in the empty box?

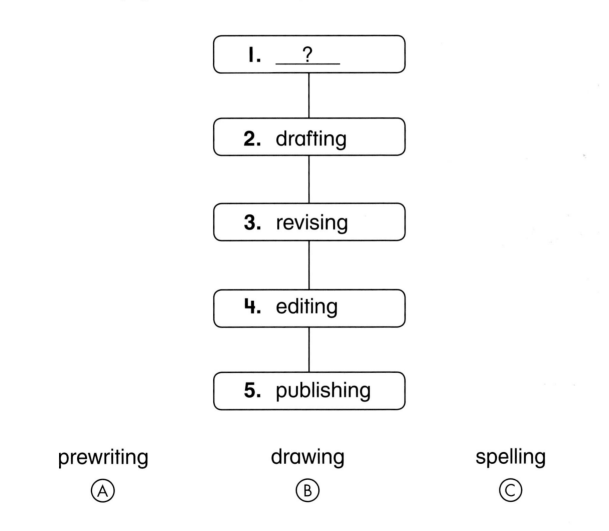

| 1. ____?____ |
| 2. drafting |
| 3. revising |
| 4. editing |
| 5. publishing |

prewriting   drawing   spelling
   Ⓐ   Ⓑ   Ⓒ

13. Which word has the same beginning sound as **sheep**?

chill	wish	shop
Ⓐ	Ⓑ	Ⓒ

Read the lines from "Asha in the Attic." Answer questions 14 and 15.

> Now, for the first time ever, Asha had the attic all to herself. It had never looked so big or so dusty or so full of stuff from the olden days.
>
> It had never looked so lonely, either. Asha felt a shiver along her spine.

14. Where could a person see pictures of old times?

   Ⓐ   in a clothing store

   Ⓑ   in a zoo

   Ⓒ   in a library book

15. When might you feel a shiver along your spine?

   Ⓐ   when feeling scared

   Ⓑ   when feeling sleepy

   Ⓒ   when feeling sad

Student _____ Date _____

Student Theme Progress Test Record

Skills Tested	Item Numbers (cross out numbers for items answered incorrectly)	Student Score	Criterion Score	If the student scored less than the Criterion Score, use these Reteaching Tools:
Comprehension Make Connections	4 9 14 15	_____ of 4	3 / 4	**Make Connections:** Comprehension Bridge 1
Target Skill Distinguish Fantasy from Reality	6	_____ of 1	1 / 1	**Distinguish Fantasy from Reality:** Teacher's Guide p. 20
Vocabulary	1 10	_____ of 2	2 / 2	**Vocabulary:** During independent reading time, review student's Vocabulary Journal and discuss how to improve the journal entries
Phonics *ph, sh, th, ch* Digraphs	8 13	_____ of 2	1 / 2	*ph, sh, th, ch* **Digraphs:** Whole Class Charts p. 4 Teacher's Guide p. 8
Short Vowels	2 11	_____ of 2	1 / 2	**Short Vowels:** Whole Class Charts p. 9 Teacher's Guide p. 24
Writing: Process Writing Organizational Pattern: Sequence	7	_____ of 1	1 / 1	**Organizational Pattern: Sequence:** Writing Chart 2, 3 Writing Bridge 2
Process: Writing Process: Introduction	12	_____ of 1	1 / 1	**Process: Writing Process: Introduction:** Writing Chart 1 Writing Bridge 1
Writing: Grammar Simple Sentences: Beginning/Ending Punctuation, Word Order, Complete Thought	3	_____ of 1	1 / 1	**Simple Sentences:** Writing Resource Guide p. 1 Writer's Handbook pp. 4–5
Subject: Naming Parts of a Sentence	5	_____ of 1	1 / 1	**Subject:** Writing Resource Guide p. 2 Writer's Handbook p. 4
		_____ / 15	12 / 15	

Answer Key

1. B   2. C   3. A   4. A   5. B   6. A   7. C   8. B   9. C   10. B

11. B   12. A   13. C   14. C   15. A

THEME ② Ongoing Test Practice

Sample
Read the story. Fill in the circle next to your answer.

Ants on a Log

What makes a good snack? How about ants on a log? No, you do not go outside to find it. You can make it in your kitchen.

Fill a piece of celery with peanut butter. Set raisins in the peanut butter. The raisins look like ants walking on a peanut butter log.

S. What would the kitchen smell like while you make this snack?

Ⓐ   trees

Ⓑ   flowers

Ⓒ   peanut butter

Fill in the circle next to your answer.

I. Which two words rhyme?

Ⓐ   bake, make

Ⓑ   make, mine

Ⓒ   bail, back

Read the story. Fill in the circle next to your answer.

A Change in the Living Room

Rico stopped at Ms. Garza's garden. "Your roses are very pretty," Rico said.

"Would you like some?" Ms. Garza asked. Together, Rico and Ms. Garza picked some roses. They were red, yellow, pink, and white.

When Rico got home, he got out a tall blue vase. He filled it with water and put the roses in. He put the roses in the living room. They made the room brighter.

2. Which picture shows what Rico did?

    Ⓐ   Ⓑ   Ⓒ

3. What did Rico's living room probably smell like?

    oranges   cookies   flowers
      Ⓐ   Ⓑ   Ⓒ

4. Choose the word that goes on the line.

Rico's mother said, "Long ago, the white rose was a
_____ of love."

    sound   symbol   smell
      Ⓐ   Ⓑ   Ⓒ

Name _____ Date _____

Fill in the circle next to your answer.

1. Which word has the same ending sounds as **rain**?

    stain   rake   nap
    Ⓐ   Ⓑ   Ⓒ

2. What does the word <u>role</u> mean?

    At school, the teacher's <u>role</u> is to teach children.

    Ⓐ list

    Ⓑ desk

    Ⓒ job

3. Which of these is a correct sentence?

    Ⓐ Claire and her brother running.

    Ⓑ Claire and her brother run.

    Ⓒ Claire and her brother runs.

4. Read the lines from "Hello! I'm Paty."

> Maribel, Lupe, and I are making *papel picado*. That means cut paper banners. We will use them to decorate for the party.

Which picture shows what the girls made?

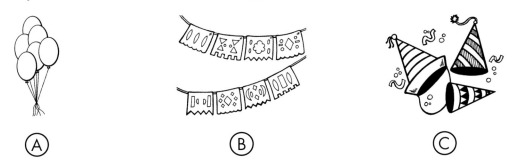

Ⓐ   Ⓑ   Ⓒ

5. Read the lines from "Home, Sweet Home."

> I gaze on the moon
> As I tread the dark wild,
> And feel that my mother
> Now thinks of her child.

Where do you look to see the moon?

Ⓐ   in the sky

Ⓑ   in the grass

Ⓒ   under a tree

6. What is in a report?

Ⓐ rhymes

Ⓑ make-believe animals

Ⓒ facts

7. Read the sentence.

| Evan and Mom cooked soup. |

What is the telling part of the sentence?

Ⓐ cooked soup

Ⓑ Evan

Ⓒ and

8. Which word rhymes with the picture word?

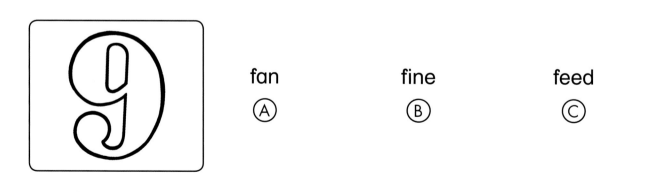

fan   fine   feed
Ⓐ   Ⓑ   Ⓒ

9. Read the sentences.

> I will never forget my first day of school
> First I was late to school
> Then I got lost and sat down in a third grade classroom

What does the writer need to do to these sentences?

Ⓐ   Make a clear point.

Ⓑ   Add end marks.

Ⓒ   Put ideas in order.

10. Which picture word has the same ending sounds as **cute**?

Ⓐ   Ⓑ   Ⓒ

11. Choose the word that goes on the line.

Joe is Mary's brother. He is her _____ .

(A) sibling

(B) member

(C) identity

12. Which two words rhyme?

(A) away, today

(B) toad, today

(C) after, away

Read the lines from "Hello! I'm Paty." Answer questions 13, 14, and 15.

> We each try to hit and break the piñata with a stick. My family and friends clap and shout. When the piñata breaks, all the goodies fly out! After the piñata breaks, we all eat lunch together.

13. What might you hear when Paty and her friends try to hit the piñata?

soft whispers   angry voices   happy shouts

Ⓐ   Ⓑ   Ⓒ

14. When else do people clap and shout?

Ⓐ   when going to bed

Ⓑ   when watching a baseball game

Ⓒ   when studying in a library

15. How do Paty's family and friends feel?

Ⓐ   alone

Ⓑ   sad

Ⓒ   excited

Student _____   Date _____

Student Theme Progress Test Record

Skills Tested	Item Numbers (cross out numbers for items answered incorrectly)	Student Score	Criterion Score	If the student scored less than the Criterion Score, use these Reteaching Tools:
Comprehension Create Images	4 13 15	_____ of 3	2 / 3	**Create Images:** Comprehension Bridge 2
Make Connections	5 14	_____ of 2	2 / 2	**Make Connections:** Comprehension Bridge 1
Vocabulary	2 11	_____ of 2	1 / 2	**Vocabulary:** During independent reading time, review student's Vocabulary Journal and discuss how to improve the journal entries
Phonics *ake, ine, oke, ute* Word Families	8 10	_____ of 2	1 / 2	*ake, ine, oke, ute* **Word Families:** Whole Class Charts p. 13 Teacher's Guide p. 40
ail, ain, ay Word Families	1 12	_____ of 2	1 / 2	*ail, ain, ay* **Word Families:** Whole Class Charts p. 18 Teacher's Guide p. 56
Writing: Process Writing Form: Report	6	_____ of 1	1 / 1	**Form: Report:** Writing Chart 5, 6 Writing Bridge 4
Trait: Writing Traits: Introduction	9	_____ of 1	1 / 1	**Trait: Writing Traits: Introduction:** Writing Chart 4 Writing Bridge 3
Writing: Grammar Predicate: Telling Part of a Sentence	7	_____ of 1	1 / 1	**Predicate:** Writing Resource Guide p. 3 Writer's Handbook p. 4
Subject-Verb Agreement	3	_____ of 1	1 / 1	**Subject-Verb Agreement:** Writing Resource Guide p. 4 Writer's Handbook p. 5
		_____ / 15	11 / 15	

Answer Key

1. A   2. C   3. B   4. B   5. A   6. C   7. A   8. B   9. B   10. C

11. A   12. A   13. C   14. B   15. C

Name _____ Date _____

Sample
Read the story. Fill in the circle next to your answer.

Saturday Mornings

Every Saturday morning, Mato's family gets up early. They get in the truck and drive around. They look for signs that say "Yard Sale" or "Garage Sale." They look at things people are trying to sell. Sometimes they find things they need.

S. What can you ask to learn more about Mato's Saturday mornings?

Ⓐ What does Mato's family do on Sundays?

Ⓑ Where does Mato go to school?

Ⓒ How early do Mato and his family get up?

Fill in the circle next to your answer.

I. Which picture word has the same ending sounds as **float**?

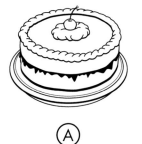
Ⓐ

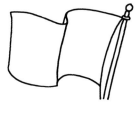
Ⓑ

Ⓒ

Read the story. Fill in the circle next to your answer.

Aunt Mavis

All of my aunts are alike, except Aunt Mavis. My aunts live in houses. They have children who are my cousins. Aunt Mavis does not live in a house. She lives in a camper. Aunt Mavis drives to different places and writes about the places in her <u>journal</u>. She does not stay in motels. She just stays in her camper. She says, "I am like a hermit crab. I take my house with me."

2. Who lives in a house that moves?

Ⓐ   Aunt Mavis

Ⓑ   the cousins

Ⓒ   all the aunts

3. What does the word <u>journal</u> mean?

Ⓐ   a postcard

Ⓑ   a book to keep thoughts and ideas

Ⓒ   a map with names of roads and cities

4. What can you ask to learn more about where Aunt Mavis lives?

Ⓐ   Does Aunt Mavis like hermit crabs?

Ⓑ   How many beds are in her camper?

Ⓒ   What kind of work does Aunt Mavis do?

THEME ③ Theme Progress Test

Fill in the circle next to your answer.

I. Which two words rhyme?

Ⓐ rug, grow

Ⓑ snow, snake

Ⓒ grow, snow

2. What does the illustrator of a story do?

Ⓐ changes the title

Ⓑ draws the pictures

Ⓒ writes the story

3. Which command has the correct end mark?

Ⓐ Stephen, watch out?

Ⓑ Stephen, watch out.

Ⓒ Stephen, watch out!

4. Read the lines from "The Moon."

> But all of the things that belong to the day
> Cuddle to sleep to be out of her way;
> And flowers and children close their eyes
> Till up in the morning the sun shall arise.

Which picture shows what the children are doing?

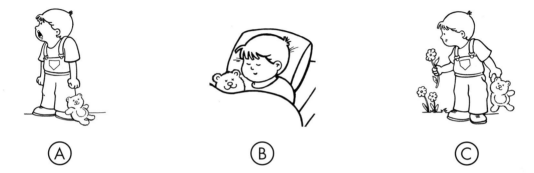

Ⓐ   Ⓑ   Ⓒ

5. Read the lines from "The Missing Moon Mystery."

> On Saturday morning, Bentley Beaver banged his tail on
> the ground. Slap, slap! "I'm having a party," he announced.
> "What kind?" asked Freda Fox.
> "A moon party," said Bentley.

What can you ask to learn more about Bentley's party?

Ⓐ   What do you do at a moon party?

Ⓑ   How big is Bentley's tail?

Ⓒ   Is Freda Fox Bentley's best friend?

6. What things are found in **all** stories?

(A) characters, cars, and mysteries

(B) animals, people, and a setting

(C) characters, a setting, and a plot

7. Which sentence has the correct end mark?

(A) What is today's date?

(B) What is today's date.

(C) What is today's date!

8. Which two words rhyme?

(A) west, weed

(B) weed, speed

(C) pass, speed

9. You are writing about going to school. Which idea fits with the story's point?

Going to School
I. I walk to the bus stop.
2.
3. I get off the bus at school.

(A) I like eggs and toast.

(B) I can read and write.

(C) I get on the big, yellow school bus.

10. Read the sentences.

> The big cat stretched and yawned. She sat up tall and washed her face. Then she spotted a red ball. She ran and jumped on the ball and rolled it around the room. As quickly as she started, she stopped and lay down. The big cat yawned and went back to sleep.

What is the plot of this story?

(A) A cat wakes, plays, and then sleeps.

(B) The story is about a big cat.

(C) This takes place inside a house.

11. What does the word <u>measure</u> mean?

We had to <u>measure</u> the room to get a rug that fit.

Ⓐ   to find out how big something is

Ⓑ   to see how fast something moves

Ⓒ   to change something's color

12. Read the lines from the poem "The Moon."

> The squalling cat and the squeaking mouse,
> The howling dog by the door of the house,
> The bat that lies in bed at noon,
> All love to be out by the light of the moon.

What does the bat do at noon?

Ⓐ   The bat flies.

Ⓑ   The bat sleeps.

Ⓒ   The bat howls.

13. Which word has the same ending sounds as **heat**?

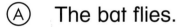

star   save   seat
Ⓐ   Ⓑ   Ⓒ

**Read the lines from "The Missing Moon Mystery." Answer
questions 14 and 15.**

> Bentley's friends played and cast shadows in the glow of the
> moon. They danced, laughed, and ate until the sun was ready
> to rise. Then everyone went home to bed.

14. What did the sky look like during the party?

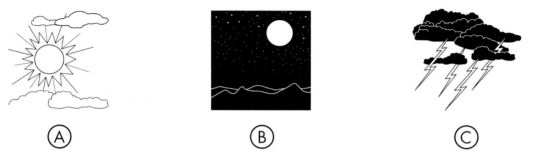

    Ⓐ   Ⓑ   Ⓒ

15. What can you ask to learn more about the party?

    Ⓐ   What food did they eat at the party?

    Ⓑ   Where did Bentley sleep after the party?

    Ⓒ   Who is Bentley's best friend?

Student _____ Date _____

THEME 3

Student Theme Progress Test Record

Skills Tested	Item Numbers (cross out numbers for items answered incorrectly)	Student Score	Criterion Score	If the student scored less than the Criterion Score, use these Reteaching Tools:
Comprehension Ask Questions	5 12 15	_____ of 3	2 / 3	**Ask Questions:** Comprehension Bridge 3
Create Images	4 14	_____ of 2	1 / 2	**Create Images:** Comprehension Bridge 2
Target Skill Identify Plot	10	_____ of 1	1 / 1	**Identify Plot:** Teacher's Guide p. 92
Understand Role of Author and Illustrator	2	_____ of 1	1 / 1	**Understand Role of Author and Illustrator:** Teacher's Guide p. 86
Vocabulary	11	_____ of 1	1 / 1	**Vocabulary:** During independent reading time, review student's Vocabulary Journal and discuss how to improve the journal entries
Phonics *eed, ea, eat* Word Families	8 13	_____ of 2	1 / 2	*eed, ea, eat* **Word Families:** Whole Class Charts p. 22 Teacher's Guide p. 74
oat, ow Word Families	1	_____ of 1	1 / 1	*oat, ow* **Word Families:** Whole Class Charts p. 27 Teacher's Guide p. 90
Writing: Process Writing Form: Story	6	_____ of 1	1 / 1	**Form: Story:** Writing Chart 8, 9 Writing Bridge 6
Trait: Ideas	9	_____ of 1	1 / 1	**Trait: Ideas:** Writing Chart 7 Writing Bridge 5
Writing: Grammar Telling and Asking Sentences with End Punctuation	7	_____ of 1	1 / 1	**Telling and Asking Sentences:** Writing Resource Guide p. 5 Writer's Handbook p. 5
Command and Expressive Sentences with End Punctuation	3	_____ of 1	1 / 1	**Command and Expressive Sentences:** Writing Resource Guide p. 6 Writer's Handbook p. 5
		_____ / 15	12 / 15	

Answer Key

1. C   2. B   3. C   4. B   5. A   6. C   7. A   8. B   9. C   10. A

11. A   12. B   13. C   14. B   15. A

Name _____ Date _____

■■ THEME ④ Ongoing Test Practice

Sample
Read the story. Fill in the circle next to your answer.

Jen's Job

This morning Jen has a job to do. She puts on her favorite red shirt and goes to school. At school Jen hooks the flag on the rope. Then she slowly pulls the rope. The flag goes up as Jen pulls down.

When Jen is done, she goes to Ms. Wong's class. She takes out her reading book and gets to work.

S. What is important about Jen's job?

    (A)   She wears a red shirt.

    (B)   She hangs the flag in front of the school.

    (C)   She is in Ms. Wong's class.

Fill in the circle next to your answer.

I. Which word has the same ending sounds as **start**?

    coat   corn   cart
    (A)   (B)   (C)

Read the story. Fill in the circle next to your answer.

How to Make a Sun Print

What can you do on a bright, sunny day? Try making a sun print. First get some dark paper. Next choose objects that will lay flat. You might use keys or small toys. Then go outside when the <u>solar</u> light is bright. Put the paper in the sun. Set the objects on top of the paper. Leave the objects and paper in the sun for a few hours. Then take the objects away. You will be able to see the shapes on the paper.

2. What materials are important for making a sun print?

   Ⓐ   dark paper and flat objects

   Ⓑ   white paper and keys

   Ⓒ   round objects and shapes

3. What does the word <u>solar</u> mean in the story?

   Ⓐ   from the sun

   Ⓑ   from the moon

   Ⓒ   from a lamp

4. Why is weather important in the story?

   Ⓐ   You must listen for the sounds that rain makes.

   Ⓑ   You must have a sunny day.

   Ⓒ   You must have cloud shapes to draw.

Name _____ Date _____

Fill in the circle next to your answer.

1. Which sentence is correct?

   Ⓐ A Spaceship landed on the Moon.

   Ⓑ A Spaceship landed on the moon.

   Ⓒ A spaceship landed on the moon.

2. Which picture shows what <u>orbit</u> means?

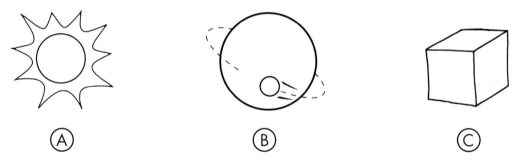

   Ⓐ   Ⓑ   Ⓒ

3. Which two words rhyme?

   Ⓐ horn, worn

   Ⓑ heat, horn

   Ⓒ wake, worn

4. Read the lines from "Super Sun Science."

> Our teacher said we could use a telescope to study sunspots without hurting our eyes. But we wouldn't look into the telescope. We would use it to create a sun picture.

What is very important when studying sunspots?

(A) keeping your eyes safe

(B) drawing a picture of the sun

(C) looking into a telescope

5. Read the lines from "What Makes Earth Hot or Cold?"

> Earth is tilted as it goes around the sun.
> Parts of Earth tilted *away* from the sun get colder.

What can you ask to learn more about these lines?

(A) What winter month has the coldest weather?

(B) What parts of Earth are water and what parts are land?

(C) What happens to the parts of Earth that are tilted toward the sun?

6. Choose the word that goes on the line.

Marita loves orange juice. She drinks a glass _____.

- (A) daily

- (B) position

- (C) rotate

7. Which word has the same ending sounds as the picture word?

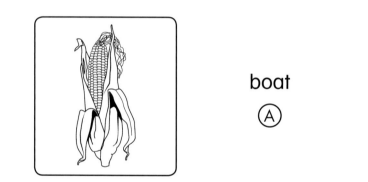

boat   beak   born
(A)   (B)   (C)

8. Which of these is an asking sentence?

- (A) We are late.

- (B) Run fast!

- (C) What time is it?

9. Which two words rhyme?

   (A)   glue, glow

   (B)   glue, due

   (C)   glue, day

10. You want to write a story about science, but you don't know where to begin. What should you do?

   (A)   Write down ideas.

   (B)   Choose a different story to write.

   (C)   Edit the story.

11. Which word has the same middle sound as **juice**?

   (A)   rice

   (B)   suit

   (C)   jail

12. Look at the web.

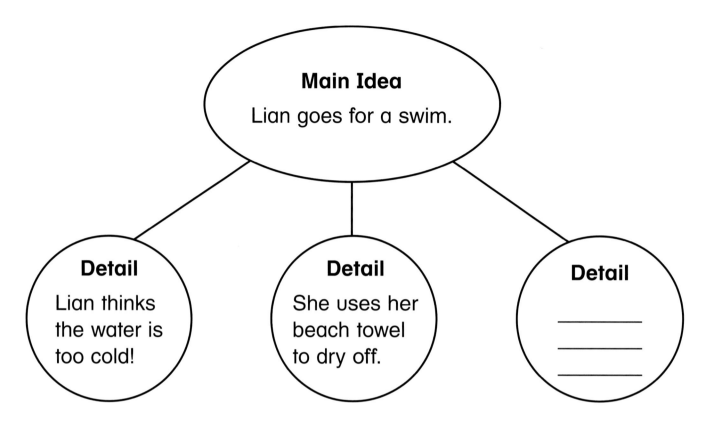

What is a good detail to add to the web?

Ⓐ Lian sits in the sun to warm up.

Ⓑ Lian signs up for soccer camp.

Ⓒ Lian helps her dad wash dishes.

Read the lines from "Super Sun Science." Answer questions 13, 14, and 15.

> The sun is important for every living thing on our planet. It gives us warmth and light. It's hotter than anything on Earth. Without the sun, Earth would freeze!
>
> The sun is at the center of our solar system.

13. Which sentence below is an important idea in these lines?

    Ⓐ   Our solar system is very big.

    Ⓑ   The sun gives light and warmth to living things.

    Ⓒ   Some areas of Earth are warmer than others.

14. What can you ask to learn more about the solar system?

    Ⓐ   What time does the sun rise?

    Ⓑ   Are plants living things?

    Ⓒ   How many planets go around the sun?

15. Why is the sun important to Earth?

    Ⓐ   The sun is very big.

    Ⓑ   The sun keeps Earth warm.

    Ⓒ   Other planets circle the sun.

Student _____ Date _____

Student Theme Progress Test Record

Skills Tested	Item Numbers (cross out numbers for items answered incorrectly)	Student Score	Criterion Score	If the student scored less than the Criterion Score, use these Reteaching Tools:
Comprehension Determine Importance	4 13 15	_____ of 3	2 / 3	**Determine Importance:** Comprehension Bridge 4
Ask Questions	5 14	_____ of 2	2 / 2	**Ask Questions:** Comprehension Bridge 3
Vocabulary	2 6	_____ of 2	1 / 2	**Vocabulary:** During independent reading time, review student's Vocabulary Journal and discuss how to improve the journal entries
Phonics *ue, ui* Vowel Patterns	9 11	_____ of 2	1 / 2	***ue, ui* Vowel Patterns:** Whole Class Charts p. 31 Teacher's Guide p. 106
or, orn, art Word Families	3 7	_____ of 2	1 / 2	***or, orn, art* Word Families:** Whole Class Charts p. 36 Teacher's Guide p. 122
Writing: Process Writing Organizational Pattern: Main Idea and Details	12	_____ of 1	1 / 1	**Organizational Pattern: Main Idea and Details:** Writing Chart 11, 12 Writing Bridge 8
Process: Prewriting	10	_____ of 1	1 / 1	**Process: Prewriting:** Writing Chart 10 Writing Bridge 7
Writing: Grammar Review Sentence Types	8	_____ of 1	1 / 1	**Sentence Types:** Writing Resource Guide p. 7 Writer's Handbook pp. 5–6
Common Nouns	1	_____ of 1	1 / 1	**Common Nouns:** Writing Resource Guide p. 8 Writer's Handbook p. 14
		_____ / 15	11 / 15	

Answer Key

1. C   2. B   3. A   4. A   5. C   6. A   7. C   8. C   9. B   10. A

11. B   12. A   13. B   14. C   15. B

Name _____ Date _____

Sample
Read the story. Fill in the circle next to your answer.

A Flying Object

Jason said, "Look! There's a spaceship outside!"

Maggie looked at the window. She could see the string that hung Jason's toy from the window above. Maggie covered her mouth so Jason would not see her laugh.

"We should run for safety," Maggie said as she kept reading her book.

S. What can you guess from the story?

Ⓐ Maggie was afraid.

Ⓑ Maggie and Jason were having fun.

Ⓒ Jason's toy was broken.

1. What does the word <u>rural</u> mean?

We visited a horse farm in a <u>rural</u> area.

country   city   kitchen
Ⓐ   Ⓑ   Ⓒ

2. Which two words rhyme?

chair, chest   fair, chair   fair, fear

Ⓐ   Ⓑ   Ⓒ

Read the passage and the questions. Then fill in the circle next to your answer.

> ### Neil Armstrong
>
> Neil Armstrong was six when he took his first ride in an airplane. He became a pilot when he was 16 years old. When he grew up, he flew jet planes.
>
> Neil was the first person to walk on the moon. He said, "That's one small step for a man, one giant leap for mankind." When he got back to Earth, there were parades. He visited 21 countries.

3. What helped Neil Armstrong learn to be an astronaut?

    Ⓐ   flying planes

    Ⓑ   traveling in many countries

    Ⓒ   walking on the moon

4. What happened after Neil Armstrong went to the moon?

    Ⓐ   He was sent right back to space.

    Ⓑ   He was kept quiet.

    Ⓒ   He was treated like a hero.

Name _____ Date _____

Fill in the circle next to your answer.

I. Which word has the same ending sound as **fir**?

   Ⓐ   stir

   Ⓑ   stop

   Ⓒ   shut

2. Which word makes the sentence correct?

      My grandmother moved to _____ last month.

   Ⓐ   arkansas

   Ⓑ   ARKANSAS

   Ⓒ   Arkansas

3. Which word rhymes with the picture name?

              egg   year   read
              Ⓐ   Ⓑ   Ⓒ

4. Which word goes on the line?

Labor Day is the first Monday in _____.

Ⓐ September

Ⓑ september

Ⓒ SEPTEMBER

5. Read the lines from "Where Is Kitty?"

> At last they crossed the bridge into the city. María was amazed by the crowded streets. Just then, Kitty jumped into her lap. "Kitty! No, no, no, Kitty! I told you to stay at home!"

What is important about these lines?

Ⓐ There is a bridge.

Ⓑ The streets were crowded.

Ⓒ Kitty should be at home.

6. Choose the word that goes on the line.

The _____ of going on the boat was to see dolphins.

(A) rural

(B) crossing

(C) purpose

7. Read the lines from "Where Is Kitty?"

> "Look around," Papa said. "He must be somewhere nearby."
> María looked under the other wagons, but Kitty wasn't there.

Who is lost?

(A) Papa

(B) Kitty

(C) María

8. Which of these is correct about writing a draft?

(A) Everything must be correct in a draft.

(B) You write a draft before you prewrite.

(C) You do not have to worry about capital letters.

9. Read the lines from "Where Is Kitty?"

> On the wagon, María thought about her lonely life growing up on the farm. In the country, all the other children lived far away. "I hope I meet a new friend in the city," she sighed.

What is María's problem?

Ⓐ She got lost going to the city.

Ⓑ She does not want to ride in a wagon.

Ⓒ She does not have any friends.

10. Read the lines from the poem "It's Loud!"

> Elephants squeal with their huge trunks,
> And bugs buzz 'round the flowers.

Which word sounds like what it means?

Ⓐ buzz

Ⓑ huge

Ⓒ bugs

11. Read the lines from "Where Is Kitty?"

> A man was standing next to a car on the side of the road. "What is that?" María asked. "It's stuck in the mud."

How do you know María lived long ago?

Ⓐ María had never seen a car before.

Ⓑ The sides of the road were muddy.

Ⓒ A man was standing by a car.

12. Which word has the same ending sounds as **burn**?

Ⓐ bark

Ⓑ turn

Ⓒ tune

13. Which two words rhyme?

Ⓐ deal, deer

Ⓑ deer, peer

Ⓒ peer, pen

Read the lines from the poem "It's Loud!" Answer questions 14 and 15.

People in the city shout,
And trains and trucks are loud.
So off we went to a nearby zoo
To get away from city crowds.

The lions roar like jumbo jets.
The bats squeak in the dark.

14. What does the author think about the city?

    Ⓐ   The city has too many animals.

    Ⓑ   The city is too noisy.

    Ⓒ   The city has too few people.

15. What is an important reason the author went to the zoo?

    Ⓐ   to get away from crowds

    Ⓑ   to hear lions roar

    Ⓒ   to watch jumbo jets

Student _____   Date _____

THEME 5

Student Theme Progress Test Record

Skills Tested	Item Numbers (cross out numbers for items answered incorrectly)	Student Score	Criterion Score	If the student scored less than the Criterion Score, use these Reteaching Tools:
Comprehension Infer	7 11 14	_____ of 3	2 / 3	**Infer:** Comprehension Bridge 5
Determine Importance	5 15	_____ of 2	1 / 2	**Determine Importance:** Comprehension Bridge 4
Target Skill Recognize Onomatopoeia	10	_____ of 1	1 / 1	**Recognize Onomatopoeia:** Teacher's Guide p. 152
Vocabulary	6	_____ of 1	1 / 1	**Vocabulary:** During independent reading time, review student's Vocabulary Journal and discuss how to improve the journal entries
Phonics *ir, urn* Word Families	1 12	_____ of 2	1 / 2	***ir, urn* Word Families:** Whole Class Charts p. 40 Teacher's Guide p. 140
air, ear, eer Word Families	3 13	_____ of 2	1 / 2	***air, ear, eer* Word Families:** Whole Class Charts p. 45 Teacher's Guide p. 156
Writing: Process Writing Organizational Pattern: Problem and Solution	9	_____ of 1	1 / 1	**Organizational Pattern: Problem and Solution:** Writing Chart 14, 15 Writing Bridge 10
Process: Drafting	8	_____ of 1	1 / 1	**Process: Drafting:** Writing Chart 13 Writing Bridge 9
Writing: Grammar Proper Nouns: People and Places	2	_____ of 1	1 / 1	**Proper Nouns: People and Places:** Writing Resource Guide p. 9 Writer's Handbook p. 12
Proper Nouns: Days, Months, Holidays	4	_____ of 1	1 / 1	**Proper Nouns: Days, Months, Holidays:** Writing Resource Guide p. 10 Writer's Handbook p. 13
		_____ / 15	11 / 15	

Answer Key

1. A	2. C	3. B	4. A	5. C	6. C	7. B	8. C	9. C	10. A
11. A	12. B	13. B	14. B	15. A					

Name _____ Date _____

Sample
Read the story. Fill in the circle next to your answer.

Flying Matthew

Matthew looked out the window and saw a bird fly by. He began to daydream.

"What if I had wings?" he thought. Matthew imagined he flew to the ocean. He pictured himself circling high above the waves. Where would his mind take him next?

S. You do not know what <u>daydream</u> means. What question can help you?

Ⓐ   What word rhymes with it?

Ⓑ   What word begins with the same letter?

Ⓒ   What small words are in it?

I. Choose the word that goes on the line.

I took a two-day _____ to see my cousins.

journey   car   rode
Ⓐ   Ⓑ   Ⓒ

2. Which word has the same ending sounds as **spare**?

span   share   seed
Ⓐ   Ⓑ   Ⓒ

Read the passage and the questions. Then fill in the circle next to your answer.

Ming's New Address

Ming moved into a new apartment. The number plate on the door said 219. Ming saw that the apartments near hers were numbered 215 and 217. She went downstairs and saw apartment 115.

"I get it!" said Ming. "Apartments on the first floor start with one. Apartments on the second floor start with two."

---

3. What helps you tell what the word <u>plate</u> means in this story?

Ⓐ   Look at the end mark.

Ⓑ   Look at the picture.

Ⓒ   Check the spelling.

4. You get stuck on the word <u>downstairs</u>. What should you do?

Read on.   Stop reading.   Spell the word.
Ⓐ   Ⓑ   Ⓒ

THEME ⑥ Theme Progress Test

Fill in the circle next to your answer.

1. Which word has the same ending sounds as **room**?

   Ⓐ blow

   Ⓑ block

   Ⓒ bloom

2. How can you write the name <u>Mister Weiss</u> shorter?

   Ⓐ Mr. Weiss

   Ⓑ mr. Weiss

   Ⓒ mr Weiss

3. Which two words rhyme?

   Ⓐ wire, wore

   Ⓑ store, wore

   Ⓒ stone, store

4. Which of these is a <u>boundary</u>?

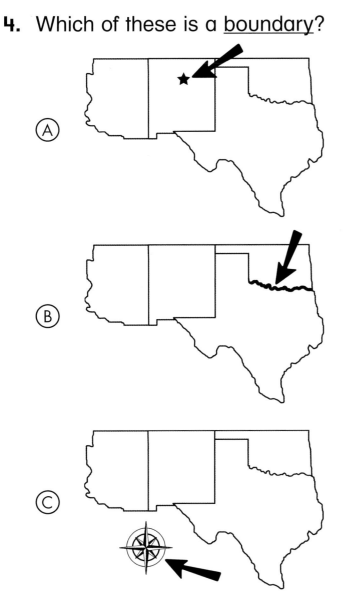

Ⓐ

Ⓑ

Ⓒ

5. Which sentence is correct?

Ⓐ My school is on Elm Street across from a park.

Ⓑ My School is on elm street across from a park.

Ⓒ My school is on elm street across from a Park.

6. Which sentence should be **first**?

   Ⓐ   Some people ride the bus.

   Ⓑ   There are two ways to travel to school.

   Ⓒ   Some people walk to school.

7. Which word has the same ending sounds as **few**?

   Ⓐ   net

   Ⓑ   nap

   Ⓒ   new

8. Read the lines from "Greetings from Route 66."

> You'd love Meramec Caverns in Missouri. They are underground paths that a man named Lester Dill discovered. The outlaw Jesse James and his gang used the caverns as a hideout back in the 1870s.

What are these lines mostly about?

   Ⓐ   Lester Dill

   Ⓑ   Jesse James

   Ⓒ   Meramec Caverns

9. Read the lines from "The Wabash Cannonball."

> Through the hills of Minnesota
> Where the rippling waters fall
> No chances can be taken
> On the Wabash Cannonball.

You get stuck on the word <u>Minnesota</u>. What should you do?

Ⓐ   Sound out the word.

Ⓑ   Find a rhyming word.

Ⓒ   Spell the word.

10. Which word has the same ending sounds as **fire**?

tire   turn   fine
Ⓐ   Ⓑ   Ⓒ

11. Choose the word that goes on the line.

Alaska is the largest _____ in our country.

Ⓐ   terrain

Ⓑ   route

Ⓒ   state

Read the lines from "Greetings from Route 66." Answer questions 12 and 13.

> The RV is a mess and the air conditioner broke. It is so hot! We've been stopping a lot at little diners to get ice-cold drinks. That helps. We just passed a house covered with hubcaps—Cool!

12. You get stuck on the words <u>air conditioner</u>. What should you do?

Ⓐ   Write the words and then spell them.

Ⓑ   Stop reading and read a different page.

Ⓒ   Read on to find clues about the meaning.

13. What can you buy at a diner?

Ⓐ   food and drink

Ⓑ   gas and maps

Ⓒ   hubcaps

Read the lines from "The Wabash Cannonball." Answer questions 14 and 15.

> Listen to the jingle,
> The rumble and the roar
> As she glides along the woodlands,
> Through hills and by the shore.
> Hear the mighty rush of the engine,
> Hear those lonesome riders squall
> While traveling through the jungle
> On the Wabash Cannonball.

14. You don't know what the word <u>woodlands</u> means. What could you do?

    Ⓐ   Look for capital letters and punctuation marks.

    Ⓑ   Break the word into two small words.

    Ⓒ   Read the lines really fast.

15. When does the Wabash Cannonball make noise?

    Ⓐ   when it is stopped

    Ⓑ   when it moves

    Ⓒ   when people get off

Student _____   Date _____

Student Theme Progress Test Record

Skills Tested	Item Numbers (cross out numbers for items answered incorrectly)	Student Score	Criterion Score	If the student scored less than the Criterion Score, use these Reteaching Tools:
Comprehension Use Fix-Up Strategies	9 12 14	_____ of 3	2 / 3	**Use Fix-Up Strategies:** Comprehension Bridge 6
Infer	13 15	_____ of 2	1 / 2	**Infer:** Comprehension Bridge 5
Vocabulary	4 11	_____ of 2	2 / 2	**Vocabulary:** During independent reading time, review student's Vocabulary Journal and discuss how to improve the journal entries
Phonics *ore, are, ire* Word Families	3 10	_____ of 2	1 / 2	***ore, are, ire* Word Families:** Whole Class Charts p. 49 Teacher's Guide p. 172
oom, ew Word Families	1 7	_____ of 2	1 / 2	***oom, ew* Word Families:** Whole Class Charts p. 54 Teacher's Guide p. 188
Writing: Process Writing Organizational Pattern: Main Idea and Details	8	_____ of 1	1 / 1	**Organizational Pattern: Main Idea and Details:** Writing Chart 17, 18 Writing Bridge 12
Trait: Organization	6	_____ of 1	1 / 1	**Trait: Organization:** Writing Chart 16 Writing Bridge 11
Writing: Grammar Proper Nouns: Titles	2	_____ of 1	1 / 1	**Proper Nouns: Titles:** Writing Resource Guide p. 11 Writer's Handbook pp. 11–13
Review Common vs. Proper Nouns	5	_____ of 1	1 / 1	**Common vs. Proper Nouns:** Writing Resource Guide p. 12 Writer's Handbook pp. 12–14
		_____ / 15	11 / 15	

Answer Key

1. C   2. A   3. B   4. B   5. A   6. B   7. C   8. C   9. A   10. A

11. C   12. C   13. A   14. B   15. B

Name _____ Date _____

Sample
Read the story. Fill in the circle next to your answer.

Kayla Goes Home

Kayla presses her face against the window. At first she sees only trees. Then she sees farms. Little by little, there are more houses. Next she sees tall buildings. People are walking. Buildings are bunched together. Finally the sidewalk is filled with people. Mom pulls into a parking spot. "We're home!" she says.

S. Where does Kayla live?

on a farm   in the city   in the car
Ⓐ   Ⓑ   Ⓒ

Fill in the circle next to your answer.

1. Choose the word that goes on the line.

Loc used a _____ to cut the grass.

smile   hill   machine
Ⓐ   Ⓑ   Ⓒ

2. Which word has the same ending sounds as **lawn**?

rain
Ⓐ

late
Ⓑ

drawn
Ⓒ

Read the story. Fill in the circle next to your answer.

State Names

Each of the 50 states has a name. Did you know that each state also has a nickname? A nickname is a fun, second name.

Peaches grow in Georgia. It is the Peach State. Buckeye trees grow in Ohio. It is the Buckeye State. Kansas is the Sunflower State, and Washington is the Evergreen State.

3. What does each nickname in the story tell you?

Ⓐ   what a buckeye tree looks like

Ⓑ   something interesting about each state

Ⓒ   how to grow peaches

4. Maine is a state with many pine tree forests. What is Maine's nickname?

Pine Tree State
Ⓐ

Big Oak State
Ⓑ

Leaf State
Ⓒ

Name _____ Date _____

Fill in the circle next to your answer.

I. Which word has the same ending sounds as **talk**?

till   chalk   kite
Ⓐ   Ⓑ   Ⓒ

2. Read the story.

> One fine morning, I walked to the store. I saw Monica.
> I waved to her, but she did not see me.

Who tells this story?

Ⓐ   Monica

Ⓑ   you

Ⓒ   I

3. Choose the word that goes on the line.

The cat _____ under the bed.

hides   pillow   yellow
Ⓐ   Ⓑ   Ⓒ

4. Read the lines from "Going for a Ride."

> The key is turned—it's time to start.
> My engine hums, and we depart!

What has a key and an engine?

Ⓐ a door

Ⓑ a backpack

Ⓒ a car

5. Read the lines from "Robot-Cat."

> Robo rolled into the hall. It raced up the wall and scratched
> the wallpaper.

What should you do if you get stuck on the word <u>wallpaper</u>?

Ⓐ Skip the word.

Ⓑ Spell the word.

Ⓒ Break the word into parts.

6. What is a good greeting for a letter to Aunt Kate?

(A) Thank you so much!

(B) Dear Aunt Kate,

(C) Good-bye, Aunt Kate

7. Choose the word that goes on the line.

Luther has a brown coat. _____ coat is brown.

(A) Luther's

(B) Luthers

(C) Luther

8. Which picture name rhymes with **draw**?

(A)   (B)   (C)

9. Read the story.

> Last night I had a dream. I was making biscuits. I put them in the oven. They grew and grew and grew! The biscuits opened the oven door! Soon they filled the kitchen!
> My neighbors came over and we ate. Yum!

What kind of voice did the writer use?

(A) sad

(B) funny

(C) serious

10. Which word has the same middle sound as **haunt**?

(A) hush

(B) that

(C) caught

11. What does the word <u>labor</u> mean?

It took one day of <u>labor</u> to dig the garden.

(A) sleep

(B) work

(C) growing

12. Read the lines from "Going for a Ride."

I sit in a garage that's dark,
With my engine off and gear in park,
Until my owner needs a ride—
Then I get to drive outside!

What happens first in the poem?

(A) The car sits in the garage.

(B) The car drives outside.

(C) The owner needs a ride.

Read the lines from "Robot-Cat." Answer questions 13, 14, and 15.

> "The noise probably woke Mom and Dad. Quick, help me fix Robo before they come downstairs," said Paula.
> They opened Robo's panels and put its parts back inside. Paula snapped the motor in place. Robo's eyes lit up.

13. How do you know the girls fixed Robo?

Ⓐ Robo's eyes lit up.

Ⓑ Robo's motor snapped.

Ⓒ Robo's panels opened.

14. What does the picture help you understand?

Ⓐ Robo belongs to Dad.

Ⓑ Robo cost a lot.

Ⓒ Robo is a toy cat.

15. What were Mom and Dad doing before the noise?

shopping   sleeping   cooking
   Ⓐ   Ⓑ   Ⓒ

Student _____   Date _____

Student Theme Progress Test Record

Skills Tested	Item Numbers (cross out numbers for items answered incorrectly)	Student Score	Criterion Score	If the student scored less than the Criterion Score, use these Reteaching Tools:
Comprehension Synthesize	4 13 15	_____ of 3	2 / 3	**Synthesize:** Comprehension Bridge 7
Use Fix-Up Strategies	5 14	_____ of 2	1 / 2	**Use Fix-Up Strategies:** Comprehension Bridge 6
Target Skill Identify Story Structure	12	_____ of 1	1 / 1	**Identify Story Structure:** Teacher's Guide p. 224
Identify Point of View	2	_____ of 1	1 / 1	**Identify Point of View:** Teacher's Guide p. 218
Vocabulary	11	_____ of 1	1 / 1	**Vocabulary:** During independent reading time, review student's Vocabulary Journal and discuss how to improve the journal entries
Phonics *au, aw, awn* Vowel Patterns	8 10	_____ of 2	1 / 2	***au, aw, awn* Vowel Patterns:** Whole Class Charts p. 58 Teacher's Guide p. 206
alk, all Word Families	1	_____ of 1	1 / 1	***alk, all* Word Families:** Whole Class Charts p. 63 Teacher's Guide p. 222
Writing: Process Writing Form: Letter	6	_____ of 1	1 / 1	**Form: Letter:** Writing Chart 20, 21 Writing Bridge 14
Trait: Voice	9	_____ of 1	1 / 1	**Trait: Voice:** Writing Chart 19 Writing Bridge 13
Writing: Grammar Possessive Nouns	7	_____ of 1	1 / 1	**Possessive Nouns:** Writing Resource Guide p. 13 Writer's Handbook p. 10
Action Verbs	3	_____ of 1	1 / 1	**Action Verbs:** Writing Resource Guide p. 14 Writer's Handbook pp. 15–16
		_____ / 15	12 / 15	

Answer Key

1. B	2. C	3. A	4. C	5. C
6. B	7. A	8. A	9. B	10. C
11. B	12. A	13. A	14. C	15. B

Name _____ Date _____

Sample
Read the story. Fill in the circle next to your answer.

A Great Tool

Dad put a nail in the wall. The nail was too high.

"We need a tool to get the nail out," said Dad. He picked up the hammer. "This is a great tool. I can use it to pull the nail out."

"Wow," said Carlos. "The hammer sure made the work easy!"

S. Why did Dad pull the nail out of the wall?

Ⓐ   He put the nail too high.

Ⓑ   Carlos wanted to put the nail in the wall.

Ⓒ   The nail was broken.

Fill in the circle next to your answer.

1. Which word has the same ending sounds as the picture name?

short   bath   shook
Ⓐ   Ⓑ   Ⓒ

Read the story. Fill in the circle next to your answer.

Ella's Old Dresses

Grandma cut Ella's old dresses into square pieces. Ella asked what she was doing.

"I am making a quilt," Grandma said. She got out her sewing machine and showed Ella how to push on the pedal to make it run. She showed her how to sew the squares together. Soon the old dresses became a colorful quilt!

2. Why did Grandma cut up Ella's old dresses?

   (A)　She wanted to use the dresses to make a quilt.

   (B)　She wanted Ella to get some new dresses.

   (C)　She wanted to learn how to sew.

3. Choose the word that goes on the line.

   Grandma showed Ella how to _____ a sewing machine.

clean	cut	operate
(A)	(B)	(C)

4. What can you tell about quilts?

   (A)　They are round.

   (B)　They are made of cloth.

   (C)　They are heavy.

THEME ⑧ Theme Progress Test

Fill in the circle next to your answer.

1. Which two words rhyme?

   Ⓐ bank, bump

   Ⓑ back, best

   Ⓒ brink, blink

2. Read the lines from "Presenting: Amazing Magnets."

   > You can make puppets to act out your play, just like real actors!
   > You can use magnets to make your puppet actors move. The
   > magnets stay hidden underneath a stage you can make.

   What do you use the magnets for?

   Ⓐ to make puppets move

   Ⓑ to make puppets talk

   Ⓒ to make puppets laugh

3. Read the sentence.

> Tony builds a model plane.

Which word in the sentence is an action word?

Ⓐ builds

Ⓑ plane

Ⓒ Tony

4. Which word has the same ending sounds as **wood**?

ring	stood	phone
Ⓐ	Ⓑ	Ⓒ

5. Choose the word that goes on the line.

Sheep are eating in the grassy _____.

Ⓐ attract

Ⓑ magnet

Ⓒ field

6. Which sentence should the writer start with?

(A) Finally cover and water the seeds.

(B) Next drop three seeds in the hole.

(C) First dig a small hole in the dirt.

7. Choose the word that goes on the line.

Sara _____ happy that her team won.

(A) were

(B) am

(C) was

8. Which picture word rhymes with **trunk**?

(A)   (B)   (C)

9. Read the story. The sentences are numbered.

> ### The Bus Ride
>
> (1) Devon got on the bus. (2) He sat in the third seat with Marcus. (3) Suddenly, the bus left the ground and started flying! (4) Devon had eggs and toast for breakfast. (5) The bus landed on the roof of the school!

Which sentence does not belong?

sentence 1   sentence 4   sentence 5
Ⓐ   Ⓑ   Ⓒ

10. Which word has the same ending sounds as **crook**?

look   late   lawn
Ⓐ   Ⓑ   Ⓒ

11. What does the word <u>object</u> mean?

The teacher held up an <u>object</u> and asked the class what it was.

Ⓐ   something you can see and touch

Ⓑ   something you cannot have

Ⓒ   something with no shape

Read the lines from "Magnets Are Amazing Tools." Answer questions 12 and 13.

> Magnets come in many shapes and sizes. Some magnets are very strong! Magnets are in things we use every day.

12. What does the picture help you understand?

Ⓐ Magnets are used in televisions.

Ⓑ Magnets used on refrigerators are small.

Ⓒ Some magnets are strong enough to pick up cars.

13. How can a magnet help a person work?

Ⓐ It can be made into large shapes.

Ⓑ It can pick up heavy things.

Ⓒ It can be fun to play with.

Read the lines from "Presenting: Amazing Magnets." Answer questions 14 and 15.

> This is because the magnet attracts the metal in the paper clip. Magnets only attract certain metals. Steel and iron are easy for a magnet to attract. Magnets cannot attract copper or brass.

14. What must paper clips be made of?

Ⓐ steel

Ⓑ brass

Ⓒ copper

15. What can a magnet attract?

Ⓐ a brass button

Ⓑ a steel nail

Ⓒ a copper coin

Student _____ Date _____

Student Theme Progress Test Record

Skills Tested	Item Numbers (cross out numbers for items answered incorrectly)	Student Score	Criterion Score	If the student scored less than the Criterion Score, use these Reteaching Tools:
Comprehension Monitor Understanding	2 12 15	_____ of 3	2 / 3	**Monitor Understanding:** Comprehension Bridge 8
Synthesize	13 14	_____ of 2	2 / 2	**Synthesize:** Comprehension Bridge 7
Vocabulary	5 11	_____ of 2	1 / 2	**Vocabulary:** During independent reading time, review student's Vocabulary Journal and discuss how to improve the journal entries
Phonics *ood, ook* Word Families	4 10	_____ of 2	1 / 2	***ood, ook* Word Families:** Whole Class Charts p. 67 Teacher's Guide p. 238
ank, ink, unk Word Families	1 8	_____ of 2	1 / 2	***ank, ink, unk* Word Families:** Whole Class Charts p. 72 Teacher's Guide p. 254
Writing: Process Writing Organizational Pattern: Sequence	6	_____ of 1	1 / 1	**Organizational Pattern: Sequence:** Writing Chart 23, 24 Writing Bridge 16
Process: Revising	9	_____ of 1	1 / 1	**Process: Revising:** Writing Chart 22 Writing Bridge 15
Writing: Grammar Linking Verbs	7	_____ of 1	1 / 1	**Linking Verbs:** Writing Resource Guide p. 15 Writer's Handbook p. 16
Review Action and Linking Verbs	3	_____ of 1	1 / 1	**Action and Linking Verbs:** Writing Resource Guide p. 16 Writer's Handbook pp. 15–16
		_____ / 15	11 / 15	

Answer Key

1. C   2. A   3. A   4. B   5. C   6. C   7. C   8. B   9. B   10. A

11. A   12. C   13. B   14. A   15. B

MID-YEAR REVIEW

Read the story. Fill in the circle next to your answer.

Dear Allison,

    Thank you so much for the paint set. What a great holiday gift! I can't wait to use it. I think I will paint a picture of us. I will show it to you at our dance class with Miss Jo. Do you think Miss Jo will be our teacher next year, too?

    Again, I love the paint set. We can use it when you come over next Friday. We can pick you up after school. My mom said you live near my school. Then we can drive to my house and paint!

Your friend,
Lilly

I. How do Allison and Lilly know each other?

Ⓐ   They are sisters.

Ⓑ   They are in dance class together.

Ⓒ   They are neighbors.

2. When might you write a thank-you letter to a friend?

  Ⓐ when a friend helps you with some work

  Ⓑ when a friend breaks your bike

  Ⓒ when a friend isn't feeling well

3. Who is telling about the holiday gift she got?

  Ⓐ Miss Jo

  Ⓑ Lilly

  Ⓒ Allison

4. What is the greeting in this letter?

  Ⓐ Your friend,

  Ⓑ Lilly

  Ⓒ Dear Allison,

5. Why did Allison give Lilly the paint set?

  Ⓐ It was a holiday gift.

  Ⓑ It was Lilly's birthday.

  Ⓒ Allison was moving away.

74 *Mid-Year Review*

Read the story. Fill in the circle next to your answer.

Mr. Green's Garden

Mr. Green lived in a building in the city. "I want to look out my window and see flowers like the ones in the park," said Mr. Green. "I will plant some flowers in pots."

Mr. Green opened his window. He put out pots with dirt in them. As he sprinkled the seeds, a big wind came along. Mr. Green watered the pots and closed the window.

Mr. Green watched and waited. But no flowers grew in his pots.

Then one day, Mr. Green walked up to his building. Flowers were growing in cracks in the sidewalk. They were the kind of flowers he had planted in his pots. Mr. Green laughed, "So I WILL get to see flowers!"

6. Why did the flowers grow in the sidewalk?

Ⓐ Mr. Green watered the sidewalk.

Ⓑ The wind blew Mr. Green's seeds into the cracks.

Ⓒ Mr. Green put the pots on the sidewalk.

7. What did it probably smell like in front of Mr. Green's building?

a farm
Ⓐ

soap
Ⓑ

fresh flowers
Ⓒ

8. Which word has the same ending sounds as **seed**?

will
Ⓐ

what
Ⓑ

weed
Ⓒ

9. What happens first in the story?

Ⓐ Mr. Green waters the pots.

Ⓑ Mr. Green puts dirt in the pots.

Ⓒ Mr. Green waits for flowers to grow.

10. Choose the word that goes on the line.

Mr. Green lives in a building in an _____ area.

urban
Ⓐ

interval
Ⓑ

exploration
Ⓒ

Read the story. Fill in the circle next to your answer.

Just Say Moo in Maryland!

What kind of drink comes with a school lunch? Milk often does. Many children drink milk several times each day.

Milk is the state drink of Maryland. That is because Maryland has quite a few dairy farms. This is where milk cows are raised.

Most milk cows in Maryland are a kind of cow called Holsteins. They have large black and white spots. The pattern of spots is different on each cow.

Every day, each one of these cows can drink 30 to 40 gallons of water. That is about the same as a full bathtub. And one cow can eat about 80 pounds of feed! But each cow can give eight gallons of milk a day. That is about 100 glasses!

---

11. What important thing comes from cows?

water   milk   feed
Ⓐ   Ⓑ   Ⓒ

12. Which word from the story rhymes with **gray**?

drink   day   give
Ⓐ   Ⓑ   Ⓒ

13. Which word sounds like what it means?

(A) moo

(B) drink

(C) spots

14. You get stuck on the word <u>dairy</u>. What should you do?

(A) Stop reading and read a different story.

(B) Write the word and then spell it aloud.

(C) Read on to find clues to the meaning.

15. What is the third paragraph mostly about?

(A) what Holstein cows look like

(B) how much cows eat and drink

(C) the state drink of Maryland

16. Choose the word that goes on the line.

Milk and water are two _____ drinks for children.

| position | essential | identity |
| (A) | (B) | (C) |

Read the story. Fill in the circle next to your answer.

What Is a Subway?

Most trains run above the ground. But not all trains do. Subways are trains that run under the ground. Subways travel through tunnels under city streets.

To get to a subway train, you go downstairs into the tunnel. Then you buy a ticket at the subway station. There are maps and signs to show riders which route to take.

People stand and wait for the train. When the train stops, the doors open. Some people get off, and other people get on. The subway train is a good way for people to get from one place to another in a city.

17. Why is a subway important to a city?

    Ⓐ   It helps people get around.

    Ⓑ   It runs above the ground.

    Ⓒ   It gives people exercise.

18. You want to learn more about where a subway train goes. What might you ask?

    Ⓐ   How much does a subway ticket cost?

    Ⓑ   Where can I get a subway map?

    Ⓒ   How long do I have to wait for a train?

19. Who wrote this story?

    Ⓐ   the illustrator

    Ⓑ   a subway rider

    Ⓒ   the author

20. Where does a rider buy a ticket for the subway?

    Ⓐ   on the subway train

    Ⓑ   at the underground subway station

    Ⓒ   on the street above the subway tunnel

21. What does the word route mean?

    Ⓐ   path used for travel

    Ⓑ   time between trains

    Ⓒ   cost of a ticket

Fill in the circle next to your answer.

22. What sentence would best end a story?

   Ⓐ   Finally Alex got off the bus at his grandma's house.

   Ⓑ   Next Alex got on the bus and put his money in the slot.

   Ⓒ   First the bus pulled up to Alex's bus stop.

23. Read the sentences. What is something that could really happen?

   Ⓐ   A family has a talking lamp.

   Ⓑ   A family flies on a magic carpet.

   Ⓒ   A family drives across town to shop.

24. Which two words rhyme?

      bell, yes   dear, year   day, bake
        Ⓐ   Ⓑ   Ⓒ

25. Which word has the same ending sounds as the picture word?

          pleat   jeer   dunk
           Ⓐ   Ⓑ   Ⓒ

Student _____   Date _____

Mid-Year Review Test Record

Comprehension
Cross out numbers for items answered incorrectly.

Make Connections	2	Monitor Understanding	20	
Create Images	7	Use Fix-Up Strategies	14	
Ask Questions	18	Synthesize	1	5
Determine Importance	11	Infer	6	17

If student has difficulty with Comprehension, use the Comprehension Bridges.

Total Comprehension Score _____ / 10

Target Skill

Distinguish Fantasy from Reality	23	Identify Story Structure	9
Understand Role of Author and Illustrator	19	Identify Point of View	3
Recognize Onomatopoeia	13		

If student has difficulty with Target Skills, use the Teacher's Guide lessons.

Total Target Skill Score _____ / 5

Vocabulary

10   16   21

If student has difficulty with Vocabulary, review student's Vocabulary Journal.

Total Vocabulary Score _____ / 3

Phonics

eed, ea, eat Word Families	8	*ail, ain, ay* Word Families	12
air, ear, eer Word Families	24	*ank, ink, unk* Word Families	25

If student has difficulty with Phonics, use the Whole Class Charts and Teacher's Guide lessons.

Total Phonics Score _____ / 4

Writing: Process Writing

Organizational Pattern: Sequence	22	
Organizational Pattern: Main Idea and Details	15	
Form: Letter	4	

If student has difficulty with Writing: Process Writing, use the Writing Bridges.

Total Writing: Process Writing Score _____ / 3

Total Score _____ / 25

Answer Key

1. B	2. A	3. B	4. C	5. A
6. B	7. C	8. C	9. B	10. A
11. B	12. B	13. A	14. C	15. A
16. B	17. A	18. B	19. C	20. B
21. A	22. A	23. C	24. B	25. C

Name _____ Date _____

Sample
Read the story. Fill in the circle next to your answer.

Hector's Schoolwork

Hector brings home his work from school. Hector's mom looks at his papers and then hangs them on the refrigerator. She uses magnets to hold the papers. It makes Hector feel good to see his work hanging up.

S. Where is another place you might see schoolwork hanging up?

Ⓐ on the floor

Ⓑ in a classroom

Ⓒ on a child's shirt

Fill in the circle next to your answer.

1. Which two words rhyme?

Ⓐ note, boat

Ⓑ need, bed

Ⓒ nail, ban

Read the story. Fill in the circle next to your answer.

How to Make Refrigerator Magnets

You can make your own refrigerator magnets. Cut out pictures of things you like. Make sure each picture is the size of a stamp. Paste each picture to a cardboard square. Then paste the cardboard to a small magnet and <u>wait</u> for it to dry. The magnet will stick to the refrigerator.

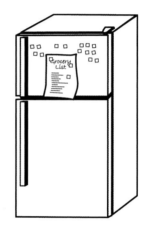

2. Where do people have refrigerators?

   Ⓐ   in their kitchen

   Ⓑ   in their bedroom

   Ⓒ   in their car

3. What does the word <u>wait</u> mean?

   Ⓐ   to add more of something

   Ⓑ   to be ready for something to happen

   Ⓒ   to finish first

4. How might you use your refrigerator magnet?

   Ⓐ   to keep things cold

   Ⓑ   to color pictures

   Ⓒ   to hang a drawing

Name _____ Date _____

THEME 9 Theme Progress Test

Fill in the circle next to your answer.

I. What does the word <u>election</u> mean?

   After the <u>election</u>, we had a new class president.

   (A) a time when people go on vacation

   (B) a time when people buy fruits and vegetables

   (C) a time when people vote

2. Which word makes the sentence correct?

   Yesterday Mary Ann and I _____ a fun game.

   (A) plays

   (B) played

   (C) playing

3. Which word has the same ending sounds as **page**?

   stage   stamp   steer
    (A)   (B)   (C)

4. Read the lines from "Grace for President!"

> STUDENT REPORTER: And the new president is Grace Molina!
> NARRATOR: Everyone cheers. Ben congratulates Grace.

What is another time that people cheer?

(A) when they watch sports

(B) when they are sad

(C) when they fall asleep

5. Read the lines from "Our Class Pet."

> To choose a pet for our whole class,
> Today we had a vote.
> We all wrote down our favorites
> In folded, secret notes.

How do you know this is a poem?

(A) It has capital letters.

(B) It talks about a pet.

(C) It has rhythm and rhyme.

6. Choose the word that goes on the line.

Patrick _____ eaten a big lunch. He is full.

(A) have

(B) has

(C) is

7. Which two words rhyme?

(A) rice, rake

(B) slice, rice

(C) sink, slice

8. What is one of the steps of editing?

(A) Check for correct spelling.

(B) Think of a story idea.

(C) Write a draft of your story.

9. Read the poem.

One, two,
Buckle my shoe.
Three, four,
Shut the door.

Which words in this poem rhyme?

Ⓐ four, door

Ⓑ one, two

Ⓒ shoe, door

10. Which word rhymes with the picture name?

pick   morn   mice

Ⓐ   Ⓑ   Ⓒ

11. Which word has the same ending sounds as **large**?

(A) bag

(B) link

(C) charge

Read the lines from "Grace for President!" Answer questions 12 and 13.

> NARRATOR: Later that day, Grace goes to her P.E. class. Grace notices something about the balls and jump ropes.
> GRACE: All the equipment is old and worn out. We can't play any sports! This stuff needs to be replaced.

12. What equipment do children use in P.E. class?

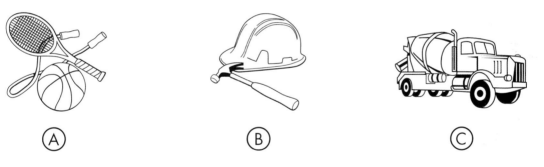

(A)   (B)   (C)

13. Why does Grace say they can't play any sports?

(A) She doesn't like her P.E. class.

(B) The equipment is old and worn out.

(C) She can't find the balls and jump ropes.

Read the lines from "Our Class Pet." Answer questions 14 and 15.

> I wanted a tarantula.
> A snake was Billy's wish.
> Steven said we need a frog.
> But most were votes for fish!

14. Which animal did most people want?

   (A)   frog

   (B)   snake

   (C)   fish

15. Which other animal could be a classroom pet?

  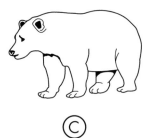

   (A)   (B)   (C)

THEME 9

Student Theme Progress Test Record

Skills Tested	Item Numbers (cross out numbers for items answered incorrectly)	Student Score	Criterion Score	If the student scored less than the Criterion Score, use these Reteaching Tools:
Comprehension Make Connections: Text to Text, Self, and World	4 12 15	_____ of 3	2 / 3	**Make Connections: Text to Text, Self, and World:** Comprehension Bridge 9
Monitor Understanding	13 14	_____ of 2	1 / 2	**Monitor Understanding:** Comprehension Bridge 8
Target Skill Recognize Rhythm and Rhyme	9	_____ of 1	1 / 1	**Recognize Rhythm and Rhyme:** Teacher's Guide p. 284
Vocabulary	1	_____ of 1	1 / 1	**Vocabulary:** During independent reading time, review student's Vocabulary Journal and discuss how to improve the journal entries
Phonics *ice* Word Family	7 10	_____ of 2	1 / 2	***ice* Word Family:** Whole Class Charts p. 76 Teacher's Guide p. 272
age, arge Word Families	3 11	_____ of 2	1 / 2	***age, arge* Word Families:** Whole Class Charts p. 81 Teacher's Guide p. 288
Writing: **Process Writing** Form: Poem	5	_____ of 1	1 / 1	**Form: Poem:** Writing Chart 26, 27 Writing Bridge 18
Process: Editing	8	_____ of 1	1 / 1	**Process: Editing:** Writing Chart 25 Writing Bridge 17
Writing: Grammar Verbs: Past and Present	2	_____ of 1	1 / 1	**Verbs: Past and Present:** Writing Resource Guide p. 17 Writer's Handbook p. 15
Helping Verbs: *has, have, had*	6	_____ of 1	1 / 1	**Helping Verbs: *has, have, had*:** Writing Resource Guide p. 18 Writer's Handbook p. 16
		_____ / 15	11 / 15	

Answer Key

1. C   2. B   3. A   4. A   5. C   6. B   7. B   8. A   9. A   10. C

11. C   12. A   13. B   14. C   15. B

Name _____ Date _____

Sample
Read the story and look at the picture. Fill in the circle next to your answer.

Asad Does His Best

Asad finished playing the song. He sat still. Then he heard clapping. It grew louder. It sounded like a roar. Asad stood and bowed.

S. Look at the picture. Which picture of Asad might you have in your mind?

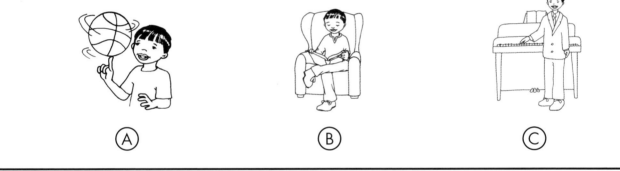

    Ⓐ   Ⓑ   Ⓒ

Fill in the circle next to your answer.

1. Which word has the same ending sounds as **mound**?

    fire   fawn   found
    Ⓐ   Ⓑ   Ⓒ

                                         Ongoing Test Practice

Read the story and look at the picture. Fill in the circle next to your answer.

Mimi's Surprise

Mimi's mom loves to have a garden in the spring. But this year she is too busy. Mimi has an idea. She asks Dad for help.

"I would love to <u>participate</u>!" says Dad. Together they dig, rake, and pull weeds in the backyard. Then they plant some seeds. Mimi smiles, "Mom will love our surprise!"

2. How might Mimi and Dad be dressed in this story?

   Ⓐ   Ⓑ   Ⓒ

3. What does the word <u>participate</u> mean?

   Ⓐ   to do something in a hurry

   Ⓑ   to take part in something

   Ⓒ   to surprise someone

4. Based on the picture above, what is something that will grow in Mimi and Dad's garden?

   Ⓐ   Ⓑ   Ⓒ

Name _____ Date _____

THEME ⑩ Theme Progress Test

Fill in the circle next to your answer.

1. Which two words rhyme?

   Ⓐ trout, true

   Ⓑ scout, scare

   Ⓒ scout, trout

2. Choose the words that go on the line.

   Liliana _____ frogs and turtles at the river.

   Ⓐ have saw

   Ⓑ has seen

   Ⓒ had seeing

3. Which word has the same ending sounds as **soil**?

   brow   brain   broil
   Ⓐ   Ⓑ   Ⓒ

4. Read the lines from "Pass It On." Look at the picture.

> Carla thought the cleanup team was a good idea. "How does your group work?"
>
> "We get together every May to clean a new river," said Jenny. "We fill lots of trash bags each year."

Which picture shows the river after the cleanup team is done?

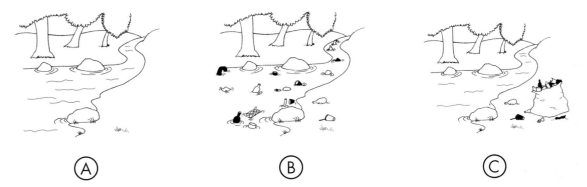

Ⓐ   Ⓑ   Ⓒ

5. Choose the word that goes on the line.

Travis _____ to the movies last night.

Ⓐ went

Ⓑ go

Ⓒ gone

6. Which word has the same ending sound as **toy**?

(A) toe

(B) joy

(C) fry

7. Read the story.

> Michael wants a sandwich. He gets out peanut butter and bread. But he can't find a knife to spread the peanut butter. He can only find a spoon and a fork.

What could you write to solve Michael's problem?

(A) He puts jelly on his sandwich, too.

(B) He doesn't have a knife.

(C) He uses the back of the spoon to spread the peanut butter.

8. Which word has the same ending sound as **cow**?

(A) what

(B) now

(C) cop

9. Karen is writing a story about her pet fish. Which sentences use the best describing words?

(A) My pet fish is shiny and blue. It is tiny, but it has big eyes that make me laugh.

(B) My pet fish is small. It is blue.

(C) My pet fish is tiny. It has two eyes and two fins. It swims in a bowl.

10. Which two words rhyme?

(A) punch, pound

(B) pound, round

(C) pool, round

Read the lines from the song "The More We Get Together" and look at the picture. Answer questions 11 and 12.

> Oh, the more we get together,
> Together, together,
> Oh, the more we get together,
> The happier we'll be.

11. How does the picture help you better understand the song?

   Ⓐ   It tells you how to sing the song.

   Ⓑ   It helps you know the names of the people.

   Ⓒ   It shows you what the people do when they are together.

12. When do children often get together?

   Ⓐ   when getting ready for bed

   Ⓑ   when reading in the library

   Ⓒ   when playing on the playground

Read the lines from "Pass It On" and look at the picture. Answer questions 13, 14, and 15.

> The next day, Eman went to the school and asked how she could help. The principal thanked her and asked her to read to Ms. García's class.

13. Which picture below shows the principal?

    Ⓐ   Ⓑ   Ⓒ

14. Choose the word that goes on the line.

Eman works at the school, but she does not get paid. She is a school _____.

    police   volunteer   emergency

    Ⓐ   Ⓑ   Ⓒ

15. Who usually reads to children at school?

Ⓐ   a teacher

Ⓑ   a cook

Ⓒ   a baby

Student _____ Date _____

THEME 10

Student Theme Progress Test Record

Skills Tested	Item Numbers (cross out numbers for items answered incorrectly)	Student Score	Criterion Score	If the student scored less than the Criterion Score, use these Reteaching Tools:
Comprehension Create Images: Use Visuals	4 11 13	_____ of 3	2 / 3	**Create Images: Use Visuals:** Comprehension Bridge 10
Make Connections: Text to Text, Self, and World	12 15	_____ of 2	1 / 2	**Make Connections: Text to Text, Self, and World** Comprehension Bridge 9
Vocabulary	14	_____ of 1	1 / 1	**Vocabulary:** During independent reading time, review student's Vocabulary Journal and discuss how to improve the journal entries
Phonics *oil, oy* Word Families	3 6	_____ of 2	1 / 2	***oil, oy* Word Families:** Whole Class Charts p. 85 Teacher's Guide p. 304
ound, out, ow Word Families	1 8 10	_____ of 3	2 / 3	***ound, out, ow* Word Families:** Whole Class Charts p. 90 Teacher's Guide p. 320
Writing: Process Writing Organizational Pattern: Problem and Solution	7	_____ of 1	1 / 1	**Organizational Pattern: Problem and Solution:** Writing Chart 29, 30 Writing Bridge 20
Trait: Word Choice	9	_____ of 1	1 / 1	**Trait: Word Choice:** Writing Chart 28 Writing Bridge 19
Writing: Grammar Irregular Verbs: *see, give, come, run, go, do*	5	_____ of 1	1 / 1	**Irregular Verbs: *see, give, come, run, go, do*:** Writing Resource Guide p. 19 Writer's Handbook p. 16
Review Helping and Irregular Verbs	2	_____ of 1	1 / 1	**Helping and Irregular Verbs:** Writing Resource Guide p. 20 Writer's Handbook p. 16
		_____ / 15	11 / 15	

Answer Key

1. C   2. B   3. C   4. A   5. A   6. B   7. C   8. B   9. A   10. B

11. C   12. C   13. B   14. B   15. A

THEME ⑪ Ongoing Test Practice

Sample
Read the story. Fill in the circle next to your answer.

Meet Louis Sachar

When Louis Sachar was in high school, he said that he wanted to write books. But he worked other jobs first. He sold cleaning products. He worked in a school. His school job led him to write the *Wayside School* books. He is known for writing *Holes* and other children's books.

S. Why did the author write this story?

Ⓐ to teach about a children's author

Ⓑ to tell a funny story

Ⓒ to write about animals

Fill in the circle next to your answer.

1. Which word has the same beginning sound as **nice**?

knock   ground   write
Ⓐ   Ⓑ   Ⓒ

Read the story. Fill in the circle next to your answer.

The Boy and the Nuts
(adapted from Aesop)

A boy put his hand into a jar to get some <u>various</u> nuts. He got a great big fistful. But with a full fist, he couldn't get his hand out of the jar. The boy began to cry. He did not want to give up any nuts, but he could not get them all out at once. His mother said, "Be happy with half the nuts and you will be able to get your hand out."

2. What is the author trying to say in this story?

   Ⓐ   Do not eat nuts.

   Ⓑ   Do not listen to your mother.

   Ⓒ   Do not try to do too much at once.

3. What does the word <u>various</u> mean in this story?

   Ⓐ   heavy

   Ⓑ   different kinds

   Ⓒ   very small

4. What is the author's purpose in telling this story?

   Ⓐ   to tell a funny story

   Ⓑ   to entertain with a scary story

   Ⓒ   to teach a lesson

THEME ⑪ Theme Progress Test

Fill in the circle next to your answer.

I. Which contraction is made from the two words **do not**?

do'nt
Ⓐ

d'not
Ⓑ

don't
Ⓒ

2. Read the sentences.

> Hannah ran a long race. Her face is as red as an apple!

What does the sentence "Her face is as red as an apple!" mean?

Ⓐ Hannah's face is the same color as an apple.

Ⓑ Hannah has on bright red lipstick.

Ⓒ Hannah likes to eat apples after she races.

3. Which word goes on the line?

Grandpa plants seeds. _____ grows beans and squash.

Ⓐ We

Ⓑ He

Ⓒ They

4. Read the lines from "At the Break of Day." Look at the picture.

> Rising with the sun's first ray,
> The farmer wakes each summer day.

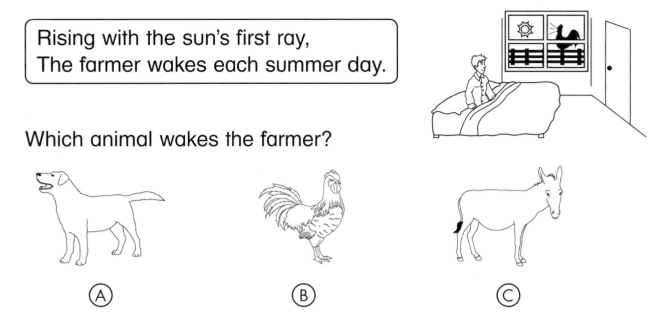

Which animal wakes the farmer?

(A)   (B)   (C)

5. Read the lines from "The Great Watermelon Contest."

> Sara built a tall fence to hide her prize watermelon. Paul hired an elephant to keep people from spying on his prize watermelon!

Why does the author write this part of the story?

(A) to teach about elephants that spy on others

(B) to show how to build a tall fence

(C) to tell how Sara and Paul keep their watermelons a secret

6. Look at the chart about cats and dogs. Which detail goes on the lines?

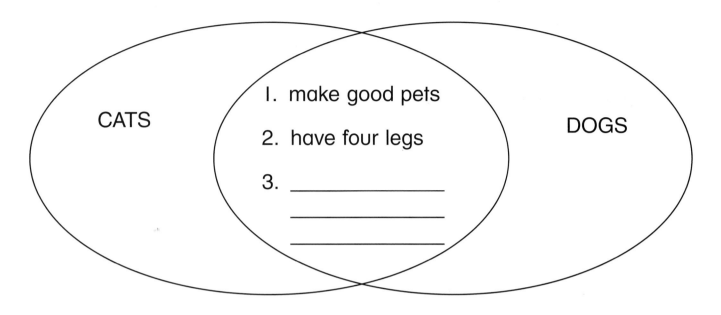

CATS

1. make good pets

2. have four legs

3. _____

_____

_____

DOGS

Ⓐ have a tail

Ⓑ purr when they're happy

Ⓒ are called puppies when they're young

7. Which word goes on the line?

Where are my gloves? I think I lost _____.

Ⓐ their

Ⓑ they

Ⓒ them

8. Which word has the same beginning sound as **now**?

  Ⓐ knot

  Ⓑ wink

  Ⓒ king

9. Read the sentences. They are numbered.

> (1) Angie's hat blew into a pond. (2) Angie waded into the water. (3) Angie grabbed her hat before a duck got it. (4) Angie laughed and put the hat on her head.

How could you change Sentence 2 to make the story sound better?

  Ⓐ change the period to a question mark

  Ⓑ change *Angie* to *She*

  Ⓒ add the word *Finally* at the beginning

10. How do you know when a story is funny?

  Ⓐ It has a main idea and details.

  Ⓑ It makes a reader laugh or smile.

  Ⓒ It uses the words *first* and *next*.

11. Which word goes on the line?

Tony eats healthful snacks. He will be _____ by eating them.

(A) nourished

(B) maintained

(C) produced

12. Read the lines from the poem "At the Break of Day."

With crops to plant and eggs to count,
He'll surely work a great amount.
He's just as busy as a bee
Growing food for you and me.

Why does the author write this poem about a farmer?

(A) to tell about the work a farmer does

(B) to tell a funny story about farmers and bees

(C) to teach how farmers grow crops

13. Which word has the same beginning sound as **right**?

won't   tire   wrong
(A)   (B)   (C)

Read the lines from "The Great Watermelon Contest" and look at the picture. Answer questions 14 and 15.

> Only one person could win first prize, so each neighbor began a secret plan to grow the winning watermelon.
> What was Anna doing with pieces of cloth and glue? What was Sara doing with a measuring tape? What was Paul doing with such large boxes?

14. What does the picture help you understand?

    Ⓐ   that Anna is covering her watermelon with cloth

    Ⓑ   that Sara is using the measuring tape to measure a watermelon

    Ⓒ   that Paul is hiding his watermelon in a big box

15. Why does the author ask about what Anna, Sara, and Paul are doing?

    Ⓐ   to show that their work is a secret

    Ⓑ   to show they don't really want to win the contest

    Ⓒ   to show that Sara's work is the best

Student _____ Date _____

THEME 11

Student Theme Progress Test Record

Skills Tested	Item Numbers (cross out numbers for items answered incorrectly)	Student Score	Criterion Score	If the student scored less than the Criterion Score, use these Reteaching Tools:
Comprehension Ask Questions: Author's Purpose	5 12 15	____ of 3	2 / 3	**Ask Questions: Author's Purpose:** Comprehension Bridge 11
Create Images: Use Visuals	4 14	____ of 2	1 / 2	**Create Images: Use Visuals:** Comprehension Bridge 10
Target Skills Understand Humor	10	____ of 1	1 / 1	**Understand Humor:** Teacher's Guide p. 356
Understand Simile	2	____ of 1	1 / 1	**Understand Simile:** Teacher's Guide p. 350
Vocabulary	11	____ of 1	1 / 1	**Vocabulary:** During independent reading time, review student's Vocabulary Journal and discuss how to improve the journal entries
Phonics Contractions	1	____ of 1	1 / 1	**Contractions:** Whole Class Charts p. 94 Teacher's Guide p. 338
kn, wr Consonant Patterns	8 13	____ of 2	1 / 2	***kn, wr* Consonant Patterns:** Whole Class Charts p. 99 Teacher's Guide p. 354
Writing: Process Writing Organizational Pattern: Compare and Contrast	6	____ of 1	1 / 1	**Organizational Pattern: Compare and Contrast:** Writing Chart 32, 33 Writing Bridge 22
Trait: Sentence Fluency	9	____ of 1	1 / 1	**Trait: Sentence Fluency:** Writing Chart 31 Writing Bridge 21
Writing: Grammar Personal Pronouns (Singular and Plural)	3	____ of 1	1 / 1	**Personal Pronouns (Singular and Plural):** Writing Resource Guide p. 21 Writer's Handbook p. 17
Subject and Object Pronouns	7	____ of 1	1 / 1	**Subject and Object Pronouns:** Writing Resource Guide p. 22 Writer's Handbook p. 17
		____ / 15	12 / 15	

Answer Key

1. C   2. A   3. B   4. B   5. C   6. A   7. C   8. A   9. B   10. B

11. A   12. A   13. C   14. B   15. A

THEME 12 Ongoing Test Practice

Sample
Read the passage. Fill in the circle next to your answer.

At the Farm

Ms. Jackson teaches second grade. Her class visited a farm. The farmer showed the class many things. First the class saw rows and rows of corn. Then they saw cows being milked. Lastly the children rode in a wagon full of hay pulled behind a tractor. Ms. Jackson's class had fun.

S. Which detail tells you about the farmer showing the class many things?

Ⓐ The class saw rows and rows of corn.

Ⓑ Ms. Jackson teaches second grade.

Ⓒ Ms. Jackson's class had fun.

I. Which word has the same ending sound as **itch**?

catch   wash   trunk
 Ⓐ   Ⓑ   Ⓒ

Read the story. Fill in the circle next to your answer.

Frida Learns to Paint

Frida Kahlo was a famous painter. But she didn't start out as a painter. She wanted to be a doctor. One day she was riding on a bus. The bus crashed and Frida was hurt. She had to stay in bed for over a year. Frida taught herself to paint. Frida painted pictures about her life. She painted pictures of herself. She used bright colors to show her life in Mexico.

Today pictures of Frida's paintings are <u>available</u> on postcards.

2. Which detail tells about Frida becoming a painter?

   Ⓐ   She wanted to be a doctor.

   Ⓑ   She taught herself to paint.

   Ⓒ   She was in a bus crash.

3. What does the word <u>available</u> mean in this passage?

   brightly colored   made smaller   can be gotten
          Ⓐ   Ⓑ   Ⓒ

4. What is this story mostly about?

   Ⓐ   Frida riding a bus

   Ⓑ   Frida working as a doctor

   Ⓒ   Frida painting

THEME 12 Theme Progress Test

Fill in the circle next to your answer.

1. Which word goes on the line?

   Jessica is a funny girl. _____ tells good jokes.

They	She	Her
Ⓐ	Ⓑ	Ⓒ

2. Look at the picture.

   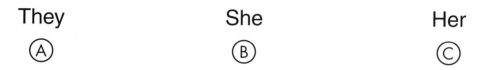

   What is the setting?

   Ⓐ   an apple farm

   Ⓑ   a barn

   Ⓒ   a city park

3. Which word goes on the line?

   An egg is _____ than a watermelon.

small	smaller	smallest
Ⓐ	Ⓑ	Ⓒ

4. Read the lines from "A Breakfast Story."

> How many people does it take to put breakfast on the table? The answer is not one or two. It may take as many as one hundred! Many people grow food, process it, move it, and sell it. Each food you consume has its own story to tell.

Which detail tells about how your food gets to you?

Ⓐ   It takes more than one or two people to put breakfast on the table.

Ⓑ   Cereal and fruit are good breakfast foods.

Ⓒ   You eat breakfast at a table.

5. Read the lines from "Food's Long Journey."

> Much of the food we eat is raised on farms. It is hard work harvesting crops and preparing them to sell.

Why did the author write this story?

Ⓐ   to entertain

Ⓑ   to teach

Ⓒ   to ask a question

6. Which word goes on the line?

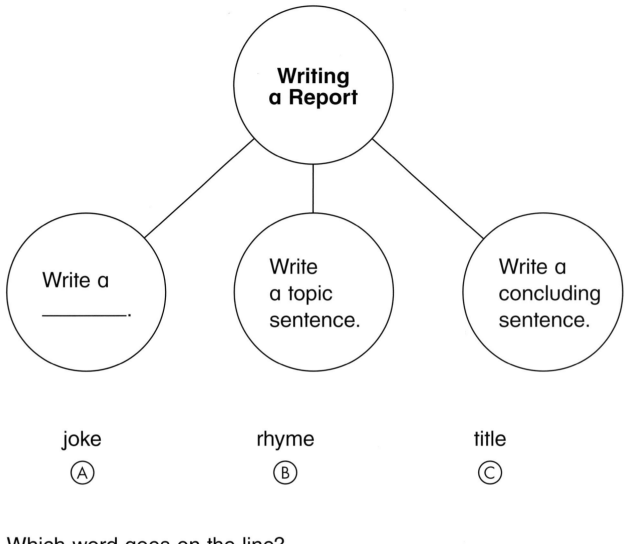

joke
(A)

rhyme
(B)

title
(C)

7. Which word goes on the line?

The skates belong to me. They are _____.

(A) my

(B) their

(C) mine

8. Which word has the same ending sound as **fudge**?

(A) edge

(B) found

(C) chalk

9. To complete your writing project, you follow the steps to publishing. What is publishing?

(A) writing a draft of a story

(B) sharing your writing with others

(C) fixing your spelling mistakes

10. Which two words have the same ending sound?

(A) fetch, flash

(B) hedge, catch

(C) pitch, batch

11. Choose the word that goes on the line.

First Mr. Wong will divide the books into piles. Then he will _____ them to different classrooms.

Ⓐ consume

Ⓑ distribute

Ⓒ range

12. Which word goes on the line?

This is the _____ apple I've ever had!

Ⓐ sweetest

Ⓑ unsweet

Ⓒ sweeter

Read the lines from "A Breakfast Story." Answer questions 13, 14, and 15.

> The milk is heated to kill germs. Then the milk goes into jugs. Soon the jugs are packed to ship. All of this happens very quickly. The fresher the milk is, the better it tastes.
> A dairy plant may have its own trucks to distribute milk to the stores.

13. Which detail tells about getting milk ready to ship?

Ⓐ Milk is put into jugs.

Ⓑ Trucks from dairy plants are big.

Ⓒ Milk tastes good when it is fresh.

14. Why did the author write these lines?

Ⓐ to tell a funny story about milk

Ⓑ to show how milk is good for you

Ⓒ to teach what happens to milk at a dairy plant

15. What detail tells you about the main idea of these lines?

Ⓐ Trucks also deliver orange juice to stores.

Ⓑ Milk jugs are tightly closed to keep out germs.

Ⓒ There are many dairy plants in the United States.

THEME 12

Student Theme Progress Test Record

Skills Tested	Item Numbers (cross out numbers for items answered incorrectly)	Student Score	Criterion Score	If the student scored less than the Criterion Score, use these Reteaching Tools:
Comprehension Determine Importance: Supporting Details	4 13 15	_____ of 3	2 / 3	**Determine Importance: Supporting Details:** Comprehension Bridge 12
Ask Questions: Author's Purpose	5 14	_____ of 2	1 / 2	**Ask Questions: Author's Purpose:** Comprehension Bridge 11
Target Skill Identify Setting	2	_____ of 1	1 / 1	**Identify Setting:** Teacher's Guide p. 382
Vocabulary	11	_____ of 1	1 / 1	**Vocabulary:** During independent reading time, review student's Vocabulary Journal and discuss how to improve the journal entries
Phonics *dge, tch* Consonant Patterns	8 10	_____ of 2	1 / 2	***dge, tch* Consonant Patterns:** Whole Class Charts p. 103 Teacher's Guide p. 370
Adjectives with *-er, -est*	3 12	_____ of 2	1 / 2	**Adjectives with *-er, -est*:** Whole Class Charts p. 108 Teacher's Guide p. 386
Writing: Process Writing Form: Report	6	_____ of 1	1 / 1	**Form: Report:** Writing Chart 35, 36 Writing Bridge 24
Process: Publishing	9	_____ of 1	1 / 1	**Process: Publishing:** Writing Chart 34 Writing Bridge 23
Writing: Grammar Possessive Pronouns	7	_____ of 1	1 / 1	**Possessive Pronouns:** Writing Resource Guide p. 23 Writer's Handbook p. 17
Review Pronouns	1	_____ of 1	1 / 1	**Pronouns:** Writing Resource Guide p. 24 Writer's Handbook p. 17
		_____ / 15	11 / 15	

Answer Key

1. B   2. A   3. B   4. A   5. B   6. C   7. C   8. A   9. B   10. C

11. B   12. A   13. A   14. C   15. B

THEME ⑬ Ongoing Test Practice

Sample
Read the story. Fill in the circle next to your answer.

Farmer's Markets

Many small towns have farmer's markets. Farmers take the vegetables that they grow and set them on tables. People who live in the city visit the market. They are happy to buy the fresh vegetables.

S. Why might a farmer go to a farmer's market?

Ⓐ   because he needs a new farm truck

Ⓑ   because he wants to sell vegetables

Ⓒ   because he lives in a city

Fill in the circle next to your answer.

I. What does the word **hopeless** mean?

full of hope   without hope   more hope
    Ⓐ   Ⓑ   Ⓒ

Read the story. Fill in the circle next to your answer.

Rebecca's Shoes

Rebecca's legs felt tired, but she had to get to the library before it closed. She put on her new blue shoes and walked out her door.

Suddenly Rebecca began to run. She ran all the way to the library. She wasn't even tired! She <u>browsed</u> the books, picked a few, and ran back outside. She sat on a bench and took her right shoe off. Her right leg felt tired. She put the shoe back on, and her leg felt better. As Rebecca ran home, she decided she'd wear her blue shoes whenever she was late or felt tired.

2. What caused Rebecca to run?

her blue shoes	her tired legs	her library books
Ⓐ	Ⓑ	Ⓒ

3. Why was Rebecca's leg tired when she sat on the bench?

   Ⓐ   because she took off her shoe

   Ⓑ   because she went to the library

   Ⓒ   because her books were heavy

4. What does the word <u>browsed</u> mean in the story?

   Ⓐ   carried heavy books

   Ⓑ   ran with many books

   Ⓒ   looked at different books

Name _____   Date _____

Fill in the circle next to your answer.

I. Choose the word that goes on the line.

Edward makes ten dollars a week. He _____ the money by walking dogs.

Ⓐ value

Ⓑ spends

Ⓒ earns

2. Which word goes on the line?

_____ go with you to the football game.

Ⓐ I'll

Ⓑ I've

Ⓒ I'm

3. What does **unclear** mean?

Ⓐ in a clear way

Ⓑ not clear

Ⓒ more clear

4. Read the lines from "Seeds of Fortune."

> The older brothers faced hard times. They had been careless with their father's money and had run out. They had to trade their fine clothes for food.

Why did the brothers trade their clothes for food?

(A) They had run out of time.

(B) They had spent all their money.

(C) They didn't like their clothes.

5. Which sentence is correct?

(A) Every story has rhythm and rhyme.

(B) Every story has a beginning, a middle, and an end.

(C) Every story has a funny ending.

6. Read the sentence.

John put on his blue backpack and walked out the door.

Which word from the sentence is a describing word?

(A) walked

(B) backpack

(C) blue

7. What does the word **teacher** mean?

(A) one who teaches

(B) without teaching

(C) teach again

8. What is a step in prewriting?

(A) Write down ideas.

(B) Correct spelling mistakes.

(C) Write a long story.

9. What does the word **cheerful** mean?

Ⓐ   one who cheers

Ⓑ   without cheer

Ⓒ   full of cheer

10. Read the sentences.

> Catherine loves to read about many things. Her teacher says, "Books are the door to new ideas."

What does Catherine's teacher mean by "Books are the door to new ideas"?

Ⓐ   You can open both books and doors.

Ⓑ   Reading is fun.

Ⓒ   You can learn a lot by opening a book and reading.

Read the lines from the poem "My New Savings Account."
Answer questions 11, 12, and 13.

> With all my money, I head to the bank.
> "Can I help you?" asks the teller Frank.
> I say, "I want to keep my savings here.
> I want my money to grow every year."
> I pour out my coins. *Clink, clink, clink.*

11. What causes the sound *clink, clink, clink*?

   Ⓐ   the child pouring out her coins

   Ⓑ   the child talking to the teller Frank

   Ⓒ   the child standing in line at the bank

12. What shows you that Frank is talking?

      ?   **" "**   **,**
      Ⓐ   Ⓑ   Ⓒ

13. Which detail tells you about saving money?

   Ⓐ   "I want my money to grow every year."

   Ⓑ   "Can I help you?" asks the teller Frank.

   Ⓒ   *Clink, clink, clink.*

Read the lines from "Seeds of Fortune." Answer questions 14 and 15.

> The couple planted the seeds that night.
> The next morning the couple was amazed to see green vines covering their land. Within weeks, dozens of golden pumpkins were ready to harvest.

14. Why was the couple amazed?

  Ⓐ The vines were green.

  Ⓑ The seeds were planted at night.

  Ⓒ Plants grew overnight.

15. Which detail tells you about plants growing quickly?

  Ⓐ The couple planted seeds.

  Ⓑ Pumpkins were ready to harvest within weeks.

  Ⓒ The couple got up early in the morning.

Student _____ Date _____

 **THEME 13**

Student Theme Progress Test Record

Skills Tested	Item Numbers (cross out numbers for items answered incorrectly)	Student Score	Criterion Score	If the student scored less than the Criterion Score, use these Reteaching Tools:
Comprehension Infer: Cause and Effect	4 11 14	_____ of 3	2 / 3	**Infer: Cause and Effect:** Comprehension Bridge 13
Determine Importance: Supporting Details	13 15	_____ of 2	1 / 2	**Determine Importance: Supporting Details:** Comprehension Bridge 12
Target Skills Understand Metaphor	10	_____ of 1	1 / 1	**Understand Metaphor:** Teacher's Guide p. 422
Understand Dialogue	12	_____ of 1	1 / 1	**Understand Dialogue:** Teacher's Guide p. 416
Vocabulary	1	_____ of 1	1 / 1	**Vocabulary:** During independent reading time, review student's Vocabulary Journal and discuss how to improve the journal entries
Phonics Prefix *un-*	3	_____ of 1	1 / 1	**Prefix *un-*:** Whole Class Charts p. 112 Teacher's Guide p. 404
Suffixes *-ful, -less, -er, -ly*	7 9	_____ of 2	1 / 2	**Suffixes *-ful, -less, -er, -ly*:** Whole Class Charts p. 117 Teacher's Guide p. 420
Writing: Process Writing Form: Story	5	_____ of 1	1 / 1	**Form: Story:** Writing Chart 38, 39 Writing Bridge 26
Process: Prewriting	8	_____ of 1	1 / 1	**Process: Prewriting:** Writing Chart 37 Writing Bridge 25
Writing: Grammar Contractions	2	_____ of 1	1 / 1	**Contractions:** Writing Resource Guide p. 25 Writer's Handbook p. 10
Adjectives	6	_____ of 1	1 / 1	**Adjectives:** Writing Resource Guide p. 26 Writer's Handbook p. 18
		_____ / 15	12 / 15	

Answer Key

1. C   2. A   3. B   4. B   5. B   6. C   7. A   8. A   9. C   10. C

11. A   12. B   13. A   14. C   15. B

THEME 14 Ongoing Test Practice

Sample
Read the story. Fill in the circle next to your answer.

Kento Turns Bad into Good

Kento went outside and saw that it had snowed a lot during the night. The snow came up to his knees! It was a bad weather day. Kento got a shovel and cleaned the walk. Then he went to his neighbors' houses and shoveled their walks. Many neighbors thanked Kento and paid him. Kento turned the bad weather into a good way to make money!

S. If you get stuck on the word <u>shovel</u>, what can you do?

   Ⓐ   Look for exclamation marks.

   Ⓑ   Look at the picture.

   Ⓒ   Look for small words.

Fill in the circle next to your answer.

I. Choose the word that goes on the line.

     Ray had four _____ in his pocket.

   Ⓐ   pennys

   Ⓑ   pennies

   Ⓒ   pennyes

Read the story. Fill in the circle next to your answer.

Does a Parrot Make a Good Pet?

Many people have pet parrots, but they are not the best pets for everyone. Parrots are noisy animals. They are also messy. Parrots throw food and feathers out of their cages. Parrots need a lot of attention. They do not like to be left home alone. Parrots need lots of space. They need a space big enough to move around and stretch their wings. If these sound like good things about a pet, a parrot might be right for you.

2. You get stuck on the word <u>parrot</u>. What can help you?

the picture	the capital letters	the story title
Ⓐ	Ⓑ	Ⓒ

3. Read the first sentence in the story. Which words in the sentence have the same beginning sound?

best pets	many people	pet parrots
Ⓐ	Ⓑ	Ⓒ

4. You are not sure what the word <u>cage</u> means. What should you do?

Ⓐ Read something else.

Ⓑ Spell the word.

Ⓒ Look at the picture.

Name _____ Date _____

Fill in the circle next to your answer.

I. What does the word <u>wages</u> mean?

My mom will get higher <u>wages</u> at her new job.

      noises   pay   tastes
       Ⓐ   Ⓑ   Ⓒ

2. Which word goes on the line?

My computer is slow. Juan's computer is fast. Juan has a
_____ computer than I do.

Ⓐ   good

Ⓑ   better

Ⓒ   best

3. Which word goes on the line?

Paige planted many _____ in the front yard.

     floweres   flower's   flowers
       Ⓐ   Ⓑ   Ⓒ

4. Read the lines from the poem "There Was an Old Woman."

> She went to market
> Her eggs for to sell;
> Fol, lol, diddle, diddle, dol.

You are not sure what the word <u>market</u> means. What can you do?

Ⓐ   Look at the picture.

Ⓑ   Spell the words.

Ⓒ   Find rhyming words.

5. Read the sentences. They are numbered.

> ### Ian Eats Lunch
>
> (1) Next he placed his order.
> (2) Then he paid for his sandwich.
> (3) First Ian picked out a sandwich.
> (4) Finally he ate his sandwich.

Which sentence should start the story?

Ⓐ   (1) Next he placed his order.

Ⓑ   (2) Then he paid for his sandwich.

Ⓒ   (3) First Ian picked out a sandwich.

6. Which word in the sentence below is a describing word?

We saw a funny clown in the parade.

(A) funny

(B) clown

(C) saw

7. Choose the word that goes on the line.

She put a bunch of _____ in the bowl.

cherrys   cherry's   cherries
(A)   (B)   (C)

8. Which sentence is correct?

(A) Maggie is saving her money to bie a basketball?

(B) Maggie is saving her money to buy a basketball.

(C) Maggie is Saving hur Money to buy a Basketball

9. Choose the word that goes on the line.

Roberto will _____ for the show by practicing his song.

(A) prepare

(B) obtain

(C) business

10. Choose the word that goes on the line.

one box   two _____

(A) boxes

(B) boxs

(C) boxies

Read the lines from "Off to Work!" Answer questions 11 and 12.

> Gary does many things at his job. He orders new books. He helps his customers. He unpacks boxes of new books. Gary gets paid.

11. You get stuck on the word <u>customers</u>. What can help you?

   (A)   the picture

   (B)   the last sentence

   (C)   the word *books*

12. Why does Gary get paid?

   (A)   He sees new books.

   (B)   He does his job.

   (C)   He likes to read.

Read the lines from "There Was an Old Woman." Answer questions 13, 14, and 15.

> She went to market
> All on a market day,
> And she fell asleep
> Upon the King's Highway.
> Fol, lol, diddle, diddle, dol.

13. Which two words from the story begin with the same sound?

   (A) day, market

   (B) asleep, fell

   (C) diddle, dol

14. The old woman missed market day. Why do you think this happened?

   (A) She was on the wrong road.

   (B) She fell asleep.

   (C) She went on the wrong day.

15. Which of the following words does the picture help you understand?

day	market	asleep
(A)	(B)	(C)

THEME 14

Student Theme Progress Test Record

Skills Tested	Item Numbers (cross out numbers for items answered incorrectly)	Student Score	Criterion Score	If the student scored less than the Criterion Score, use these Reteaching Tools:
Comprehension Use Fix-Up Strategies: Pictures	4 11 15	_____ of 3	2 / 3	**Use Fix-Up Strategies: Pictures:** Comprehension Bridge 14
Infer: Cause and Effect	12 14	_____ of 2	1 / 2	**Infer: Cause and Effect:** Comprehension Bridge 13
Target Skill Recognize Alliteration	13	_____ of 1	1 / 1	**Recognize Alliteration:** Teacher's Guide p. 448
Vocabulary	1 9	_____ of 2	1 / 2	**Vocabulary:** During independent reading time, review student's Vocabulary Journal and discuss how to improve the journal entries
Phonics Plurals -s, -es	3 10	_____ of 2	1 / 2	**Plurals -s, -es:** Whole Class Charts p. 121 Teacher's Guide p. 436
Plurals -y to -ies	7	_____ of 1	1 / 1	**Plurals -y to -ies:** Whole Class Charts p. 126 Teacher's Guide p. 452
Writing: Process Writing Organizational Pattern: Sequence	5	_____ of 1	1 / 1	**Organizational Pattern: Sequence:** Writing Chart 41, 42 Writing Bridge 28
Trait: Conventions	8	_____ of 1	1 / 1	**Trait: Conventions:** Writing Chart 40 Writing Bridge 27
Writing: Grammar Comparative and Superlative Adjectives	2	_____ of 1	1 / 1	**Comparative and Superlative Adjectives:** Writing Resource Guide p. 27 Writer's Handbook p. 18
Review Adjectives	6	_____ of 1	1 / 1	**Adjectives:** Writing Resource Guide p. 28 Writer's Handbook p. 18
		_____ / 15	11 / 15	

Answer Key

1. B   2. B   3. C   4. A   5. C   6. A   7. C   8. B   9. A   10. A

11. A   12. B   13. C   14. B   15. C

THEME 15 Ongoing Test Practice

Sample
Read the story. Fill in the circle next to your answer.

David Gets Ready

This afternoon David got ready to sing in front of the whole school. He drank a lot of water. He didn't talk so he could save his voice. Right before he walked on stage, he brushed his hair.

S. What is a good summary of "David Gets Ready"?

- Ⓐ David sang on a stage.

- Ⓑ Before David sang, he drank water, didn't talk, and brushed his hair.

- Ⓒ David didn't talk so he could save his voice for his song.

Fill in the circle next to your answer.

1. What does the word <u>droplet</u> mean?

After the rain, a <u>droplet</u> hung from a spider web.

- Ⓐ type of leaf

- Ⓑ small animal

- Ⓒ tiny bit of water

2. Which sentence happened in the past?

Carol calls.   Carol is calling.   Carol called.
Ⓐ   Ⓑ   Ⓒ

Read the passage and the questions. Then fill in the circle next to your answer.

Working Dogs

Dogs make good pets, but did you know that some dogs work? Some dogs help the police find lost or hurt people. Some dogs work as service dogs. They help people who cannot see or hear. They make sure these people stay safe when they are walking around.

Never pet a dog when it is working. The dog is using its hearing, sense of smell, and sight.

---

3. What is a good summary of "Working Dogs"?

Ⓐ Working dogs help many people. They help policemen, people who cannot see, and people who cannot hear.

Ⓑ Dogs work by using their hearing. Some dogs help the police.

Ⓒ A working dog can help the police.

4. What is a good summary of the last paragraph?

Ⓐ A working dog uses sight.

Ⓑ Don't bother a dog that is working.

Ⓒ Dogs use their hearing at work.

Name _____   Date _____

Fill in the circle next to your answer.

1. Read the lines from "My Puddle."

   > There's a spot on my sidewalk
   > That dark clouds fill with rain,
   > Just like a big, old bathtub,
   > But the sidewalk has no drain.

   What caused the spot on the sidewalk?

   the bathtub   the drain   the rain
   Ⓐ   Ⓑ   Ⓒ

2. Which of these is a sentence?

   Ⓐ Tula kicked the ball.

   Ⓑ Sat on the ground.

   Ⓒ Tula over the bridge.

3. Choose the word that goes on the line.

   We rode three rides at the fair. The last ride was
   the _____.

   bumpyest   bumpiest   bumpyiest
   Ⓐ   Ⓑ   Ⓒ

4. What does the word <u>stage</u> mean?

The first <u>stage</u> in the recipe is to cut the bread.

(A) knife

(B) present

(C) step

5. Which sentence best combines these two sentences?

A rabbit ate three beets. A deer ate two carrots.

(A) A rabbit ate three beets, ate two carrots.

(B) A rabbit and a deer ate three beets ate two carrots.

(C) A rabbit ate three beets, and a deer ate two carrots.

6. What should you do to make your writing nicer for a reader?

(A) Make the writing neat.

(B) Take out the pictures.

(C) Number each line.

7. Which sentence happened in the past?

Ⓐ   Karima looks at the picture.

Ⓑ   Karima is looking at the picture.

Ⓒ   Karima looked at the picture.

8. Choose the word that goes on the line.

Today is _____ than yesterday.

     sunnyer   sunnier   sunnyier
       Ⓐ   Ⓑ   Ⓒ

9. Read the poem.

Hickory, dickory, dock,
The mouse ran up the clock.
The clock struck one,
The mouse ran down!
Hickory, dickory, dock.

Which line is repeated?

Ⓐ   The mouse ran up the clock.

Ⓑ   The clock struck one.

Ⓒ   Hickory, dickory, dock.

Read the lines from "Grandma's Ring." Answer questions 10 and 11.

> They searched in the barn, all around the farm, here and there, there and here—everywhere—but there was no gold ring.
> They searched around the snowman, but there was no gold ring.

10. What is a good summary of these lines?

Ⓐ The girls looked for the ring by the snowman.

Ⓑ The girls looked around the farm and around the snowman, but they did not find the ring.

Ⓒ The gold ring was lost.

11. What could help tell you the meaning of <u>searched</u>?

Ⓐ the picture

Ⓑ the *-ed* ending

Ⓒ the spelling of the word

Read the lines from "My Puddle." Answer questions 12 and 13.

> The birds enjoy the puddle.
> They come to take a dip.
> My friend's dog likes it, too.
> He stops to drink a sip.

12. What helps you tell what <u>take a dip</u> means?

   Ⓐ Look at all end marks.

   Ⓑ Look for small words.

   Ⓒ Look at the picture.

13. What is a good summary of these lines?

   Ⓐ Birds and a dog use the puddle.

   Ⓑ A bird can enjoy a puddle.

   Ⓒ My friend's dog likes to drink water.

Read the lines from "Grandma's Ring." Answer questions 14 and 15.

> Grandma said it was a family treasure. That's why she gave it to Rose.
> Her mother put the ring on a red ribbon that hung around Rose's neck. The ring was too big to fit on Rose's finger.

14. What characters are in this part of the story?

Ⓐ Rose and her mother

Ⓑ a ring and ribbon

Ⓒ red ribbon and Rose's finger

15. What is a good summary of these lines?

Ⓐ Grandma's ring was on a red ribbon.

Ⓑ Grandma's ring was too big, so Rose wore it around her neck.

Ⓒ Rose put a red ribbon in Grandma's hair.

Student _____ Date _____

 **THEME 15**

Student Theme Progress Test Record

Skills Tested	Item Numbers (cross out numbers for items answered incorrectly)	Student Score	Criterion Score	If the student scored less than the Criterion Score, use these Reteaching Tools:
Comprehension Synthesize: Create a Summary	10 13 15	_____ of 3	2 / 3	**Synthesize: Create a Summary:** Comprehension Bridge 15
Use Fix-Up Strategies: Pictures	11 12	_____ of 2	1 / 2	**Use Fix-Up Strategies: Pictures:** Comprehension Bridge 14
Target Skill Identify Character	14	_____ of 1	1 / 1	**Identify Character:** Teacher's Guide p. 488
Identify Repetition of Language	9	_____ of 1	1 / 1	**Identify Repetition of Language:** Teacher's Guide p. 482
Vocabulary	4	_____ of 1	1 / 1	**Vocabulary:** During independent reading time, review student's Vocabulary Journal and discuss how to improve the journal entries
Phonics -y Plus -er and -est	3 8	_____ of 2	1 / 2	**-y Plus -er and -est:** Whole Class Charts p. 130 Teacher's Guide p. 470
Verb Ending -ed	7	_____ of 1	1 / 1	**Verb Ending -ed:** Whole Class Charts p. 135 Teacher's Guide p. 486
Writing: Process Writing Organizational Pattern: Cause and Effect	1	_____ of 1	1 / 1	**Organizational Pattern: Cause and Effect:** Writing Chart 44, 45 Writing Bridge 30
Trait: Presentation	6	_____ of 1	1 / 1	**Trait: Presentation:** Writing Chart 43 Writing Bridge 29
Writing: Grammar Review Simple Sentence Structure	2	_____ of 1	1 / 1	**Simple Sentence Structure:** Writing Resource Guide p. 29 Writer's Handbook p. 6
Compound Sentences Joined with and	5	_____ of 1	1 / 1	**Compound Sentences Joined with and:** Writing Resource Guide p. 30 Writer's Handbook p. 6
		_____ / 15	12 / 15	

Answer Key

1. C   2. A   3. B   4. C   5. C   6. A   7. C   8. B   9. C   10. B

11. A   12. C   13. A   14. A   15. B

Name _____ Date _____

THEME (16) Ongoing Test Practice

Sample
Read the passage. Fill in the circle next to your answer.

A Cool Necklace

You need water, an ice-cube tray, and a long string. Set the string in an ice-cube tray. Make sure the string hangs out at each end. Fill the tray with water and put it in a freezer. When the water has frozen into ice cubes, pop your necklace out. Wear it on a hot day to cool off!

S. What should you do if you don't understand what to do with the string?

Ⓐ   Read something else.

Ⓑ   Stop and rethink.

Ⓒ   Look in a dictionary.

Fill in the circle next to your answer.

I. Choose the word that goes on the line.

Dry plants are turning brown. It feels like this _____ will never end.

Ⓐ   drought

Ⓑ   rain

Ⓒ   puddle

Read the passage and the questions. Then fill in the circle next to your answer.

Rain or Sleet?

Wet stuff is falling from the sky! Is it rain or sleet? Rain is made of drops of water, and raindrops come in different sizes.

Sleet is made of pieces of ice. It is tiny frozen raindrops. When sleet hits the ground, it bounces and makes a rapping sound. Rain can fall in all kinds of weather, but sleet can only fall when it's cold.

2. You don't understand the last sentence. What could you do?

Ⓐ   Pause and think about what cold does to water.

Ⓑ   Spell out the words *cold* and *water*.

Ⓒ   Underline each word in the sentence.

3. What could you make notes about to help you understand the story?

Ⓐ   the ground

Ⓑ   rain and sleet

Ⓒ   things that make rapping sounds

4. Which word is made of two smaller words?

weather   frozen   raindrop
Ⓐ   Ⓑ   Ⓒ

Name _____ Date _____

THEME 16 Theme Progress Test

Fill in the circle next to your answer.

1. Choose the word that goes on the line.

   In a report, _____ support the main idea.

   Ⓐ rhymes

   Ⓑ titles

   Ⓒ facts

2. Which word is made of two smaller words?

   afternoon   answer   angry
      Ⓐ   Ⓑ   Ⓒ

3. Choose the word that goes on the line.

   Where is the cat? It is _____ under the bed.

   Ⓐ hideing

   Ⓑ hiding

   Ⓒ hidding

4. What does the word <u>careless</u> mean?

The boy was <u>careless</u> to leave his skates on the stairs.

Ⓐ   not paying attention

Ⓑ   being safe

Ⓒ   important

5. Which is a compound sentence?

Ⓐ   The farmer fed the chickens, and his wife fixed the fence.

Ⓑ   The farmer fed the chickens and pigs.

Ⓒ   The farmer drove a tractor.

6. Read the sentence. It has a mistake in it.

The Teacher asked the children to line up.

Which sentence is correct?

Ⓐ   The Teacher asked the Children to line up.

Ⓑ   The teacher asked the children to line up.

Ⓒ   The Teacher asked the children to line up?

7. Which two smaller words are used to make the name of the picture?

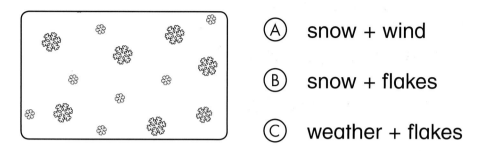

(A) snow + wind

(B) snow + flakes

(C) weather + flakes

8. Read the lines from "Splash!"

> Most of Earth's water is salt water found in the oceans. Oceans are salty because rivers flowing into the ocean bring salt from rocks and soil with them.

What should you do if you do not understand this?

(A) Find words that rhyme.

(B) Stop and make some notes.

(C) Spell each word.

9. How can you join these two sentences?

I might play a game. I might watch TV.

(A) I might play a game, or I might watch TV.

(B) I might play a game might watch TV.

(C) I might play a game, TV.

10. Choose the word that goes on the line.

The bus is _____ to pick up the children.

(A) stop

(B) stops

(C) stopping

11. Choose the word that goes on the line.

What _____ of flour do you need to make pancakes?

(A) fresh

(B) critical

(C) amount

Read the lines from "Splash!" Answer questions 12 and 13.

> The sun warms the oceans. Some heated water turns to vapor and rises into the air. The vapor cools in the air and becomes clouds. Water falls from the clouds as rain.

12. What would a good reader do if he or she does not understand what happens to vapor?

    (A) Drink more water.

    (B) Skip those sentences.

    (C) Stop and think.

13. What is a good summary of these lines?

    (A) Clouds are made by water vapor.

    (B) The sun warms water, and the water becomes vapor. Vapor becomes clouds that make rain.

    (C) When water is heated, it turns to vapor and goes into the air.

Read the lines from "Fun in the Water." Answer questions 14 and 15.

Snorkeling can be like exploring a new world. Fishing is a great way to spend time with family. Water skiers zoom across the water's surface.

14. You do not understand how snorkeling is like exploring. What could you think about to help you understand?

  Ⓐ Many people snorkel for fun.

  Ⓑ When you snorkel, you see many new plants and animals.

  Ⓒ It is smart to always snorkel with a friend.

15. Which answer below tells you what these lines are about?

  Ⓐ Fishing is not much fun, and water skiing is too fast!

  Ⓑ People like to explore new worlds.

  Ⓒ People use water to have fun. For example, people snorkel, fish, and water ski.

Student _____   Date _____

THEME 16

Student Theme Progress Test Record

Skills Tested	Item Numbers (cross out numbers for items answered incorrectly)	Student Score	Criterion Score	If the student scored less than the Criterion Score, use these Reteaching Tools:
Comprehension Monitor Understanding: Pause and Reflect	8 12 14	_____ of 3	2 / 3	**Monitor Understanding: Pause and Reflect:** Comprehension Bridge 16
Synthesize: Create a Summary	13 15	_____ of 2	1 / 2	**Synthesize: Create a Summary:** Comprehension Bridge 15
Vocabulary	4 11	_____ of 2	2 / 2	**Vocabulary:** During independent reading time, review student's Vocabulary Journal and discuss how to improve the journal entries
Phonics Verb Ending -ing	3 10	_____ of 2	1 / 2	**Verb Ending -ing:** Whole Class Charts p. 139 Teacher's Guide p. 502
Compound Words	2 7	_____ of 2	1 / 2	**Compound Words:** Whole Class Charts p. 144 Teacher's Guide p. 518
Writing: Process Writing Form: Report	1	_____ of 1	1 / 1	**Form: Report:** Writing Chart 47, 48 Writing Bridge 32
Process: Editing	6	_____ of 1	1 / 1	**Process: Editing:** Writing Chart 46 Writing Bridge 31
Writing: Grammar Other Joining Words: *but, or, so*	9	_____ of 1	1 / 1	**Other Joining Words: *but, or, so*:** Writing Resource Guide p. 31 Writer's Handbook p. 6
Review and Practice Simple vs. Compound Sentences	5	_____ of 1	1 / 1	**Simple vs. Compound Sentences:** Writing Resource Guide p. 32 Writer's Handbook p. 6
		_____ / 15	11 / 15	

Answer Key

1. C   2. A   3. B   4. A   5. A   6. B   7. B   8. B   9. A   10. C

11. C   12. C   13. B   14. B   15. C

Name _____ Date _____

Read the questions. Fill in the circle next to your answer.

1. What does the illustrator of a story do?

   (A)   write the story

   (B)   fix the spelling mistakes

   (C)   draw the pictures

2. Which word has the same ending sounds as the picture word?

              make   kite   nice
               (A)   (B)   (C)

3. Choose the word that goes on the line.

   The girl drank the grape juice. It had a delicious _____.

        taste   spend   cause
          (A)   (B)   (C)

4. Which word has the same beginning sound as **never**?

        keep   know   kite
          (A)   (B)   (C)

Read the story. Fill in the circle next to your answer.

Pancakes for Breakfast

Emily measured the flour while Uncle Josh melted the butter. Then Uncle Josh added the melted butter, baking powder, salt, and an egg to the flour. Emily stirred the batter.

"Something is wrong," Uncle Josh said. "This batter is too dry." He looked back at the recipe. "I forgot to put in the milk! These pancakes would not taste very good without milk."

Uncle Josh heated up the pan. He poured in some batter. It formed a circle. Emily sprinkled blueberries on the circle. When the batter started to bubble, Uncle Josh turned it over. The pancake was light brown.

Uncle Josh made three more pancakes. Emily helped by adding blueberries to each one.

Uncle Josh put two pancakes on each plate. Emily put a pat of butter on hers. She spread it around as it melted.

Emily took the first bite. "Uncle Josh, these are the best pancakes I've ever had!" she exclaimed.

"The blueberries make them delicious," added Uncle Josh. After that, they quietly ate their breakfast.

5. Why was the pancake batter too dry at first?

    Ⓐ   The batter needed to be stirred.

    Ⓑ   Emily added blueberries.

    Ⓒ   Uncle Josh forgot to put in the milk.

6. What is important about the blueberries?

    Ⓐ   They make the pancakes taste good.

    Ⓑ   They were grown in Emily's garden.

    Ⓒ   They are round like a pancake.

7. Who are the main characters in the story?

    Ⓐ   Uncle Josh and Emily

    Ⓑ   Emily and her brother

    Ⓒ   a cook and a boy

8. Uncle Josh burned a pancake. What could you write to tell why this happened?

    Ⓐ   Uncle Josh threw away the pancake.

    Ⓑ   Uncle Josh added more salt to the batter and stirred it in.

    Ⓒ   Uncle Josh was helping wash the blueberries. He forgot about the batter in the hot pan.

Read the story. Fill in the circle next to your answer.

A Lizard Stays Safe

Lyle Lizard's life was simple. He sat in the tree and looked for bugs. He laid in the sun and napped. Lyle had two sisters. They sometimes left the tree and went to the ground. They told Lyle about scary things on the ground, like animals much bigger than lizards! Lyle stayed in the tree. He felt safe there.

One morning Lyle sat on his favorite leaf. His green skin glowed in the sunlight. He smiled as the sun warmed him. Suddenly the sun was gone. Lyle looked up. There wasn't a cloud in the sky. What was blocking the sun?

Lyle noticed a big bird flying overhead. It was making a circle over Lyle. Suddenly Lyle felt scared. What could he do? The bird flew closer and closer.

Lyle jumped off the leaf and onto the bark of the tree. He looked around for a place to hide. Then he noticed that his foot was brown. He looked at his other feet and his tail. All of his skin was brown now! Lyle was the same color as the tree bark. The bird could not see Lyle. He looked like part of the tree!

The bird flew away. Lyle couldn't wait to tell his sisters about a good way to stay safe.

9. Lyle Lizard hid from the bird by changing colors. What else could you write to solve his problem?

(A) Lyle looked around for his sisters.

(B) Lyle hid under a big leaf until the bird flew away.

(C) Lyle saw the bird. Lyle ate a bug.

10. What detail tells about a lizard staying safe?

(A) Lyle's skin was the same color as the tree bark.

(B) Lyle saw a big bird flying above him.

(C) Lyle sat in the tree on his favorite green leaf.

11. What is the plot of this story?

(A) A lizard lives in a tree.

(B) A lizard changes color so a bird can't see him.

(C) A lizard has two sisters and sits on his favorite leaf.

12. You get stuck on the word <u>overhead</u>. What should you do?

(A) Spell the word.

(B) Stop reading.

(C) Break the word into parts.

Read the story. Fill in the circle next to your answer.

Be Smart About Snacks

Do you sometimes snack between meals? Here are some ways to be smart about snacks.

Eat only when you are hungry. Some days after school you may be as hungry as a horse. Other days you may not feel hungry at all. Make sure you have a snack because it is what your body needs.

Most of the time, just a small snack will do. Don't snack so much that you are not hungry at meals.

Eat healthful foods. These are foods that are good for you. Skip chips and candy. Try nuts, fruit, or cheese. Vegetables make great snacks, too.

The next time your parents ask if you would like a snack, say, "Yes, I would like a healthful one." Those words will be music to their ears!

13. Why did the author write this story?

    Ⓐ   to tell the reader a funny story about food

    Ⓑ   to teach the reader how to eat smart

    Ⓒ   to show the reader how to cook

14. What does the line "hungry as a horse" mean in the story?

   Ⓐ   to eat what horses eat

   Ⓑ   to be very hungry

   Ⓒ   to not eat very much

15. What might you see in your mind when you read about healthful snacks?

        Ⓐ   Ⓑ   Ⓒ

16. What does the sentence "Those words will be music to their ears!" mean in the story?

   Ⓐ   They will think you said those words too loud.

   Ⓑ   They will like hearing those words.

   Ⓒ   You will sing those words to them.

Read the story. Fill in the circle next to your answer.

Bumps

Rosa put down her book when her dad came in to say good night. Then she looked surprised. Rosa asked, "What are those bumps at the end of my bed?"

Rosa's dad laughed, "Those are your feet, silly!"

"No, they are not!" Rosa said. Rosa moved her feet. The bumps did not move.

"I'm not staying in here with whatever that is!" Rosa said. She jumped out of the bed and grabbed her dad. The bumps were still there. Rosa's dad threw back the covers. Then Rosa and her dad started to laugh.

Rosa said, "I must have forgotten that I wore my slippers in bed. My feet wiggled out, but the slippers stayed there."

Rosa got back in bed and turned off the light. "Good night, sleep tight," said her dad. "And keep those slippers in sight!"

17. Which word from the story is made of two smaller words?

    covers   slippers   bedroom

     Ⓐ   Ⓑ   Ⓒ

18. What is a good summary of the story?

Ⓐ Rosa saw strange bumps at the end of her bed. She found out the bumps were her slippers under the covers.

Ⓑ Rosa read a book. Then she took off her slippers. She went to sleep.

Ⓒ Rosa got in bed, turned off the light, and said good night to her dad.

19. What shows you that Rosa is talking?

!   " "   ?
Ⓐ   Ⓑ   Ⓒ

20. Choose the word that goes on the line.

Yesterday Rosa read three pages. Today she will _____ that number to five pages.

produce   vote   increase
Ⓐ   Ⓑ   Ⓒ

21. Which word means **no bumps**?

bumper   bumpless   bumpy
Ⓐ   Ⓑ   Ⓒ

Read the story. Fill in the circle next to your answer.

The North Wind and the Sun

"I am stronger," said the North Wind.

"No, I am stronger," said the Sun.

The two went back and forth. Suddenly a man wearing a coat walked by. This gave the Sun an idea.

"Which of us can get that man to take off his coat?" asked the Sun. "The winner is the stronger one."

The North Wind sent a cold blast toward the man. As the wind blew around him, he buttoned up his coat. The North Wind blew harder and harder. The man pulled his coat tighter and tighter.

Then the Sun began to shine. The rays were gentle and warm. The man undid the buttons on his coat. The Sun's beams grew warmer still. Finally, the man slipped off his coat and carried it.

The North Wind had been rough and harsh with the man. But the Sun had been gentle and kind. The North Wind learned that being kind would get more things done.

22. As the North Wind blew, the man said, "This is the _____ day we've had in a long time!"

windyest	windiest	windyiest
Ⓐ	Ⓑ	Ⓒ

23. Which picture shows the man after the Sun shines on him?

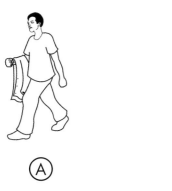

Ⓐ

Ⓑ

Ⓒ

24. Why does the man take off his coat?

Ⓐ The North Wind blows off his coat.

Ⓑ The man wants to be the strongest.

Ⓒ The Sun makes him feel warm.

25. Which word means the opposite of **to button**?

unbutton   buttonless   buttons

Ⓐ   Ⓑ   Ⓒ

26. What might you wear on a cold, windy day?

Ⓐ a warm hat

Ⓑ a bathing suit

Ⓒ shorts

Read the poem. Fill in the circle next to your answer.

The Storm

The trees swayed
As the wind blew.
I watched from my window.
I had quite a view!

Lightning flashed,
And rain fell down.
The thunder crashed.
I thought the grass would drown!

But now the sun is shining.
The sky is bright blue.
I can play in the <u>puddles</u>.
The bad weather is through!

---

27. You do not understand <u>trees swayed</u>. What should you do?

Ⓐ   Find words that rhyme.

Ⓑ   Stop and think about what you read.

Ⓒ   Look at the punctuation marks.

28. Where is a good place to be during a rainstorm?

  (A) on the playground

  (B) in the backyard

  (C) inside the house

29. How do you know this passage is a poem?

  (A) It ends with an exclamation mark.

  (B) It has rhythm and rhyme.

  (C) It describes thunder.

30. What does the word <u>puddles</u> mean?

  (A) kinds of trees

  (B) playground swings

  (C) small pools of water

31. Which words in the poem rhyme?

  (A) swayed, window

  (B) blew, view

  (C) would, drown

Read the story. Fill in the circle next to your answer.

Make Your Own Music

Do you like to listen to music? How would you like to make your own music? It can be fun to play an instrument. With very little <u>effort</u>, you can make your own. It's simple!

What You Need
empty coffee cans with lids
pencil
beans

Make a Shaker

1. Have an adult check to make sure there are no sharp edges at the top of the coffee can. Wash the can.

2. Put some beans in the can and put the lid on.

3. Shake the can. Try putting different things in the can such as rice or paper clips. Does your shaker make a different sound?

Make a Drum

1. Empty and wash coffee cans of different sizes.

2. Place them on a table. Bang the lids with the pencil, like a drum. Do different can sizes make different sounds? Does the wooden end of the pencil make a different sound than the eraser?

32. You can use beans and rice to make music. How else can you use beans and rice?

(A) You can use them for food.

(B) You can use them for soap.

(C) You can use them to stay warm.

33. You are not sure how to hold the shaker. What can you do?

(A) read the *What You Need* list again

(B) make a different instrument

(C) look at the picture

34. Which word from the story rhymes with **shook**?

(A) look

(B) like

(C) little

35. What does the word <u>effort</u> mean in the story?

(A) how long a job takes

(B) the energy it takes to do something

(C) what things you need to make something

END-OF-YEAR REVIEW

End-of-Year Review Test Record

Comprehension		Cross out numbers for items answered incorrectly.	
Synthesize: Create a Summary	18	Create Images: Use Visuals	23
Determine Importance	6	Make Connections	26
Determine Importance: Supporting Details	10	Monitor Understanding: Pause and Reflect	27
Use Fix-Up Strategies	12	Use Fix-Up Strategies: Pictures	33
Ask Questions: Author's Purpose	13	Make Connections: Text to Text, Self, and World	28 32
Create Images	15	Infer: Cause and Effect	5 24

If student has difficulty with Comprehension, use the Comprehension Bridges. **Total Comprehension Score** _____ / 14

Target Skills			
Understand Role of Author and Illustrator	1	Understand Metaphor	16
Identify Character	7	Understand Dialogue	19
Identify Plot	11	Recognize Rhythm and Rhyme	31
Understand Simile	14		

If student has difficulty with Target Skills, use the Teacher's Guide lessons. **Total Target Skill Score** _____ / 7

Vocabulary
3   20   30   35

If student has difficulty with Vocabulary, review student's Vocabulary Journal. **Total Vocabulary Score** _____ / 4

Phonics			
kn, wr Consonant Patterns	4	Suffixes *-ful, -less, -er, -ly*	21
ood, ook Word Families	34	Prefix *un-*	25
Compound Words	17	*ake, ine, oke, ute* Word Families	2
-y plus *-er, -est*	22		

If student has difficulty with Phonics, use the Whole Class Charts and Teacher's Guide lessons. **Total Phonics Score** _____ / 7

Writing: Process Writing			
Organizational Pattern: Cause and Effect	8	Form: Poem	29
Organizational Pattern: Problem and Solution	9		

If student has difficulty with Writing, use the Writing Bridges. **Total Writing: Process Writing Score** _____ / 3

Total Score _____ / 35

Answer Key

1. C	4. B	7. A	10. A	13. B	16. B	19. B	22. B	25. A	28. C	31. B	34. A
2. A	5. C	8. C	11. B	14. B	17. C	20. C	23. A	26. A	29. B	32. A	35. B
3. A	6. A	9. B	12. C	15. A	18. A	21. B	24. C	27. B	30. C	33. C	

High-Frequency Word Assessments

Use the High-Frequency Word Assessments to assess a child's ability to recognize and read high-frequency words for each theme.

Administer the assessment one-on-one at the end of each theme. Photocopy the page. Point to one word at a time and have the child say the word aloud. If the child stalls on a word, silently count to five and then say the word. Move on to the next word.

Use the High-Frequency Word Assessment Tracking Form on page 175 to record student progress and make notes about student responses. Record words that students didn't recognize and return to them during a future assessment.

THEME 1

our	sister	watch	fun	hill
move	river	those	farm	fast

THEME 2

hold	much	road	three	father
I'll	must	name	round	together

fell	fire	I've	never	run
sat	told	five	inside	night

say	top	food	found	isn't
once	set	tree	four	jump

only	friend	knew	open	should
show	turn	gave	last	outside

THEME 6

six	under	girl	give	laugh
own	small	almost	use	someone

THEME 7

left	let	paper	wasn't	sometimes
ground	past	soon	water	week

THEME 8

hand	let's	pick	lost	start
when	happy	lot	place	stay

which	hard	love	pretty	sun
while	head	may	pull	than

white	maybe	ready	these	why
might	ride	without	year	money

High-Frequency Word Assessment Tracking Form

Student _____

For each theme's high-frequency word assessment, record the words students did not recognize. You may want to return to missed words during the next theme's one-on-one assessment. Record notes about student responses.

Theme	Date	High-Frequency Words Missed	Notes About Student Responses	Score
1				___/10
2				___/10
3				___/10
4				___/10
5				___/10
6				___/10
7				___/10
8				___/10
9				___/10
10				___/10

Ongoing Test Practice Answer Key

Theme 1
S. C
1. C
2. B
3. A
4. B

Theme 2
S. C
1. A
2. B
3. C
4. B

Theme 3
S. C
1. C
2. A
3. B
4. B

Theme 4
S. B
1. C
2. A
3. A
4. B

Theme 5
S. B
1. A
2. B
3. A
4. C

Theme 6
S. C
1. A
2. B
3. B
4. A

Theme 7
S. B
1. C
2. C
3. B
4. A

Theme 8
S. A
1. C
2. A
3. C
4. B

Theme 9
S. B
1. A
2. A
3. B
4. C

Theme 10
S. C
1. C
2. A
3. B
4. B

Theme 11
S. A
1. A
2. C
3. B
4. C

Theme 12
S. A
1. A
2. B
3. C
4. C

Theme 13
S. B
1. B
2. A
3. A
4. C

Theme 14
S. B
1. B
2. A
3. C
4. C

Theme 15
S. B
1. C
2. C
3. A
4. B

Theme 16
S. B
1. A
2. A
3. B
4. C